PANORAMIC CHINA

PANORAMIC CHINA

Consultants: Zhao Qizheng Cai Mingzhao Zhou Mingwei Yan Youqiong
Israel Epstein Committee of Foreign Consultants:
    Howard Aster (Canada)
    Andy McKillop (United Kingdom)
    Tony McGlinchey (Australia)
    Foster Stockwell (USA)

Editorial Committee for the Series
Director: Huang Youyi
Executive Director: Xiao Xiaoming
Members: Fang Zhenghui Lin Liangqi Li Zhenguo Hu Baomin
    Shao Dong Chen Shi Hu Kaimin

Editorial Committee for This Volume
Directors: Xiao Xiaoming Li Zhenguo Zhang Dewen Zheng Ming
Deputy Directors: Duan Huicheng Ma Weijun
Members: Ou Zhide Deng Meiying Yang Anxing Wang Jin
    Hua Ying Zhang Qiongli Zhang Liyi Cao Jianming
    Zeng Jinrong Guo Jiexin

PANORAMIC CHINA

Yunnan
"Shangri–La" over the Horizon

FOREIGN LANGUAGES PRESS

First Edition 2006

Translators: Zhang Shaoning Li Yang Ouyang Weiping
Wang Qin Feng Xin
English Editors: Sue Duncan Yu Ling

ISBN 7-119-04077-4
© Foreign Languages Press, Beijing, China, 2006
Published by Foreign Languages Press
24 Baiwanzhuang Road, Beijing 100037, China
Website: http: //www.flp.com.cn
Email Address: Info@flp.com.cn
Sales@flp.com.cn
Distributed by China International Book Trading Corporation
35 Chegongzhuang Xilu, Beijing 100044, China
P. O. Box 399, Beijing, China

Printed in the People's Republic of China

Introduction

China has 23 provinces, four municipalities directly under the Central Government, five autonomous regions and two special administrative regions. Due to geographical and topographical differences and climatic variations, each area has its own unique natural scenery. The mountains in the north of the country are rugged and magnificent, the waters in the south are clear and turbulent, the Gobi in the northwest shines brilliantly in the sunlight, the hills in the southeast are often shrouded in floating fog, green waves of sorghum and soybean crops undulate over the vast fields of the northeast, and the mountains in the southwest, with sequestered villages and terraced fields, look tranquil and picturesque.

There are 56 ethnic groups in China. The Han, making up the overwhelming majority of the population, mainly live in the eastern and central parts of the country, while many ethnic groups with smaller populations live in the west. In China, all ethnic groups, regardless of size, are equal and respect each other. Each ethnic group has its own folk customs, religious beliefs and cultural traditions, and most use their own language and script. Regional autonomy is practiced in areas where ethnic minorities live in compact communities. All the ethnic groups call themselves "Chinese." They are courteous and friendly. In the ethnic-minority areas, the quiet environment, quaint buildings, exquisite fashions, unsophisticated folk customs and hospitality of the local people hold a great appeal to visitors from afar.

China boasts 5,000 years of recorded civilization and a brilliant culture. The country is home to such world-renowned cultural treasures as the Great Wall, terracotta warriors and horses of the First Emperor of the Qin Dynasty, Mogao Grottoes at Dunhuang, and Ming and Qing imperial palaces and mausoleums, and large numbers of ancient architectural masterpieces, including temples, Buddhist pagodas, residential buildings, gardens, bridges, city walls and irrigation

works. There are also cultural relics unearthed from ancient sites, including painted pottery, jade ware, bronze ware, large and ornate tombs and foundations of historical buildings, and many more as yet undiscovered. The museums of China's various provinces, municipalities and autonomous regions house thousands of cultural relics and works of art, among which are treasures rare in the world, displaying the long history of China and the splendid Chinese culture from different aspects. The strong, deep-rooted Chinese culture has always influenced the mentality and moral standards of the Chinese people, having developed continually in pace with the civilization. A careful study of today's Peking opera, kunqu opera, shadow plays, calligraphy, painting, paper-cutting, and even the flower-shaped steamed buns on the kitchen range of farmers will reveal elements of traditional Chinese culture as well as replications of the art of the past.

Like other countries of venerable age, China has suffered grievous calamities. During the century and more before the 1950s, the Chinese people made unrelenting struggles for the prosperity of the country, and national independence and liberation. A large number of insightful people and revolutionaries, cherishing all kinds of dreams for a strong China, studied the ways of the West in a quest for prosperity and strength, and borrowed the revolutionary experience of foreign countries. At last, the Communist Party of China, proceeding from the reality of China, and relying on the working people, founded a brand-new country, the People's Republic of China, in 1949. Since then, the Chinese people have made persistent efforts and explorations for the grand revitalization of the Chinese nation. The Chinese people's efforts in the past two decades and more have resulted in outstanding achievements, with rapid social progress, a well-developed economy, and a modern civilization and traditional culture enhancing each other.

It is easy to have a quick look at China's past and present, but it takes time to gain a panoramic knowledge of China. The "Panoramic China" series is meant to assist readers, especially those overseas, in this respect. Each volume in the series focuses on a province, municipality or autonomous region, describing, with illustrations, the outstanding characteristics of each area from different perspectives. Through this series, the reader will acquire knowledge of the real and vivid daily life of the local people, the colorful society and the developing economy, assisted by relevant information.

Location of Yunnan Province in China

Yunnan Province

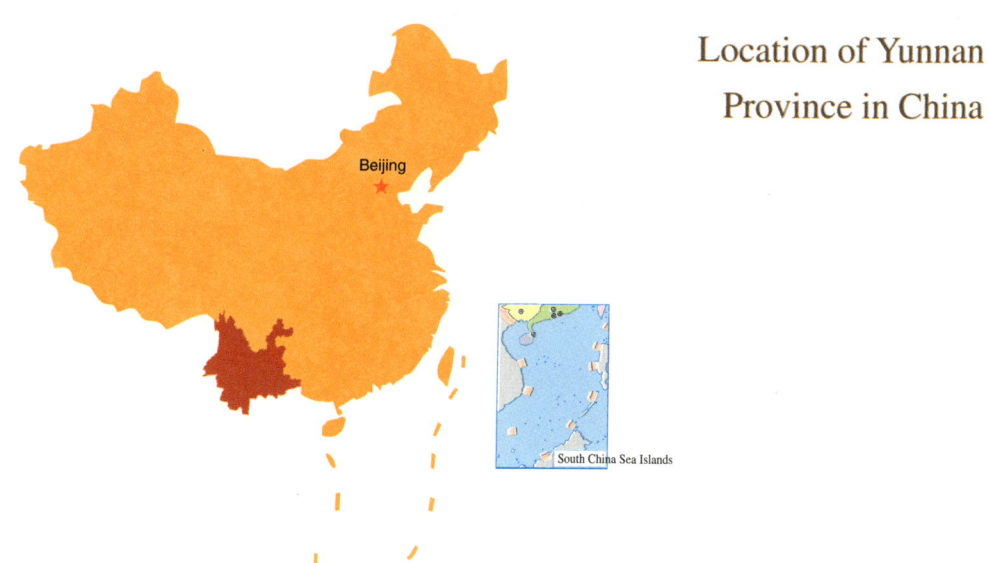

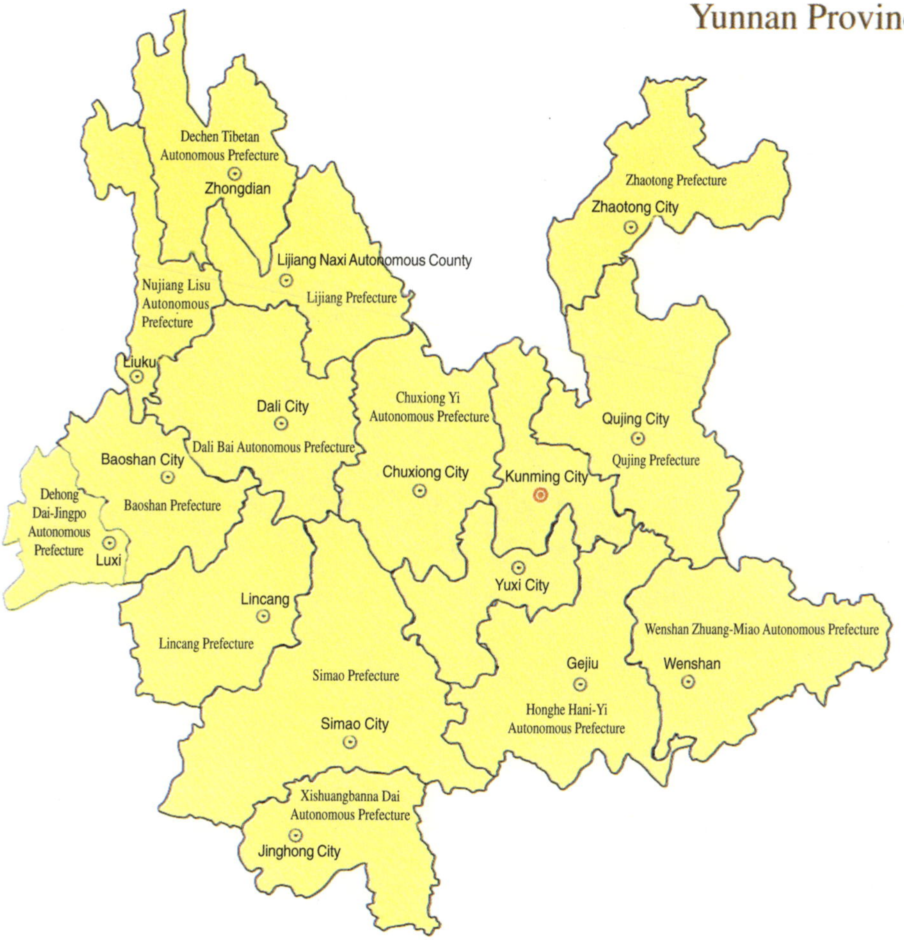

The Baimang Snow Mountain

Mosuo man on the Lugu Lake

Hani terraces and village in a sea of cloud

Getting to Know Yunnan

Yunnan, a province located in the far southwest corner of China, is a fertile and beautiful land, a land where ancient mysteries and dynamic energy combine.

Since antiquity Yunnan has been reputed as "South of the Rosy Clouds" and the "Homeland of the Rosy Clouds." Later the province has become famous for its abundant resources —wildlife, plantlife, non-ferrous metals, natural scenery, ethnic cultures, and ethnic minority music and dance. Yunnan is known to the world as the seductive Shangri-La, an imaginary utopia for which all men yearn, depicted in James Hilton' novel *Lost Horizon*.

Yunnan, one of the regions where humans first appeared and multiplied, can trace its history back 1,700,000 years, to the age of Yuanmou Man. The Neolithic Age discoveries at Zhaotong, Xichou, Lijiang, and Longtan Mountain in Chenggong, further testify to Yunnan's long history. The ancient Dian Kingdom culture that grew up between the 8th century BC and 3rd century AD (between the Spring and Autumn and the Three Kingdoms periods), the Cuan Clan culture that flourished between the 3rd and 8th centuries (Wei and Jin to mid-Tang dynasties), the Nanzhao Dali culture that thrived between the 11th and 13th centuries (mid-Song to early Yuan dynasties), and, from the Yuan Dynasty to the present day, various ethnic cultures, with Han culture as the main body... all these elements combine to create Yunnan's 2,000 year-old civilization, a civilization rich in historical and cultural resources.

Yunnan shares a 4,060 km-long border with Vietnam, Laos, and Myanmar. Since remote antiquity, people of 16 ethnic groups have been living on both sides of this long border and their frequent cross-border trade greatly boosted development on both sides of the line.

Yunnan's superb natural conditions and landscape are a delight. Agreeable climate, majestic mountains, elegant lakes, and harmony between man and Nature have won Yunnan an international reputation as an ideal tourist destination. As soon as you enter the province, you will be captivated by its clear blue skies dotted with patches of colorful clouds, its holy mountains and lakes basking in gentle sunshine, its green, green grasslands set off by white snow

mountains, its peaceful deep valleys bathed in bright moonlight, the romance of its rainforests....

Yunnan, a land of 390,000 sq km, is home to 44,000,000 people of 26 ethnic groups. Through the ages, people of all ethnic groups have lived together in solidarity and harmony, striving with energy and dynamism for common development, creating unique lifestyles and diverse cultures. Of all China's provinces Yunnan has the greatest number and most concentrated population of ethnic minority groups, and its rich ethnic diversity and multi-cultural coexistence are rare even in a world context.

These coexisting, inter-dependent cultures of Yunnan are a jewel in China's cultural crown. The precious cultural and natural heritage that Yunnan has bequeathed mankind is a vital part of the world's cultural and natural heritage. As a member of China's huge family, Yunnan has played its part in the development of the Chinese people, and also played an active role in advancing human civilization as a whole.

Yunnan's past and present alike are deserving of the world's attention and appreciation, are well worth experiencing and communicating with in person. Visit Yunnan, and you will discover the age-old past and brand-new thriving present, miraculous moving myths and vivid true reality, brilliant graceful scenery and industrious painstaking people..... they all go to make up the mysterious yet real, moving landscape of the Yunnan red earth plateau, creating this splendid land where simplicty and diversity combine.

Yunnan's extraordinary landscape is the world's common bounty. An appointment with Yunnan will bring you boundless blessings.

Whether now or in time yet to come, Yunnan will always fulfill your dreams. Yunnan, open and developing, brimming with enthusiasm and confidence, is creating an even more alluring Shangri-La, constructing an even more glorious future.

Yan Youqiong

A wonderous land whose ocher soils, rich in iron oxide, have been worked by farmers for thousands of years.

CONTENTS

Foreword /2

Hada from Buddha /15
Living in Paradise
Soul Pilgrimage
A Bird's Eye View of the
    Three Parallel Rivers
Another Sacred Place

Treasure Chest of History /53
Welcoming Bosom of the Old Town
The Ancient Tea and Horse Road
Ancient Dongba Culture
Ancient Naxi Music
Rendezvous by Lugu Lake

**Ancient Capital at a Crossroads of
    Asian Culture** /95
Between Men and Gods
Wind, Flowers, Snow, and Moon
Dali
Shibao Mountain
Menghua Town

Grand Canyon of the Orient /117
Dauntless People
Braves of Blades and Fire
Bathing in Natural Hot Springs
Sent by God

The Peacocks of Freedom /131
Last Words at Yunmen
The Peacocks of Freedom
One Hamlet Two Countries
Blessing of the Sacred Water
Religion Between Priestly and Secular
The Most Recently Confirmed Ethnic Group

The Sun's Red Girdle /169
Walking Along the Red River
The Yunnan-Vietnam Railroad
Hani Terraces
Galloping Red Bulls

World in a Gourd /193
Awa Mountains
The Mystery of the
    Cangyuan Cliff Paintings
The Warm and Spontaneous Wa
Fragrant Land

Home of Eternal Spring /211
Kunming
The West Mountain and Dianchi Lake
Meet the Great Zheng He
Visit Ashma
The Yunnan-Burma Road
    —"The Last Land Route into China"
The Flying Tigers and the Hump Route

CONTENTS

World Exposition

Mystic Land, Diverse Peoples /255

Bamei in Guangnan County—The "Peach Garden" in a Cave
Source of the Pearl River
The Yi Solar Calendar
Majestic Pass on the Wumeng Mountains
Ethnic Minorities Found Only in Yunnan

Appendixes /268

Appendix I: Ethnic Minority Festivals in Yunnan

Appendix II: Major Hotels in Yunnan

Appendix III: World Cultural and Natural Heritage Sites in Yunnan

Appendix IV: State-Level Scenic Spots in Yunnan

Appendix V: Famous State-Level Historical and Cultural Cities/Towns in Yunnan

Appendix VI: Related Websites

Y U N 云南 N A N

Foreword

"Shangri-La"

Of all China's provinces, Yunnan is the one with the largest concentration of ethnic minority peoples. It is here in Yunnan that the mingling of different ethnic groups, their ways of life and their cultures are most richly and distinctively displayed.

In 1933, the British writer James Hilton created the name "Shangri-la" in his novel Lost Horizon which is set in Yunnan, and the word came to fascinate the English-speaking world. After its publication in 1933, this mysterious novel became a world bestseller, and was adapted as a Hollywood film. Its theme tune, *Shangri-La,* enjoyed worldwide popularity.

According to Tibetans in northwest Yunnan, "Shangri-La" means "sun and moon in the heart" in the Tibetan language. Some suggest that the word was coined by Hilton for

▲ Hani village in a sea of clouds
◂ Kawagebo Snow Mountain

"香格里拉"房宁静、祥和、美丽乐净土，是团结、友爱、幸福的人间乐园。

祥和、美丽的极乐主，是团结、友爱、幸福的人间乐园。

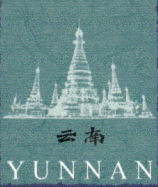

YUNNAN

his novel. But what is "Shangri-La"? Like the traditional Chinese utopia "Land of Peach Blossoms" and the West's "Garden of Eden," "Shangri-La" signifies a beautiful earthly paradise, peaceful and permeated with love and happiness.

In *Lost Horizon*, Conway of the British Consular Service and his three companions land in a Tibetan valley after their plane is hijacked, where a fascinating landscape unfolds before them — picturesque grassland, the magnificent Karakal Snow Mountain, the scent of butter drifting from lamaseries.... There are also kind-hearted, innocent Tibetan people. They are treated with great hospitality, witness miraculous things, and experience real emotional fellow-feeling with people of a different race and color, so much so that they are reluctant to leave.

As Conway continued to gaze, a deeper repose overspread him, as if the spectacle were as much for the mind as for the eye. There was hardly any stir of wind, in contrast to the upland gales that had raged the night before; the whole valley, he perceived, was a land-locked harbor, with Karakal brooding over it, lighthouse-fashion. The simile grew as he considered it, for there was actually light on the summit, an ice-blue gleam that matched the splendor it reflected. Something promoted him then to enquire the literal interpretation of the name, and Chang's answer came as a whispered echo of his own musing. "Karakal, in the valley patois, means Blue Moon," said the Chinese....

Conway was glad to find that the valley was not to be "out of bounds," though the difficulties of the descent made unescorted visits impossible. In company with Chang they all spent a whole day inspecting the green floor that was so pleasantly visible from

the cliff-edge, and to Conway, at any rate, the trip was of absorbing interest. They traveled in bamboo sedan chairs, swinging perilously over precipices while their bearers in front and to the rear picked a way nonchalantly down the steep track. It was not a route for the squeamish, but when at last they reached the lower levels of forest and foothill the supreme good fortune of the lamasery was everywhere to be realized. For the valley was nothing less than an enclosed paradise of amazing fertility, in which the vertical difference of a few

thousand feet spanned the whole gulf between temperate and tropical. Crops of usual diversity grew in profusion and contiguity, with not an inch of ground untended.... But for some chance-placed barriers, the whole valley would clearly have been a lake, nourished continually from the glacial heights around it, instead of which, a few streams dribbled through to fill reservoirs and irrigate fields and plantations....

The vast encircling massif made perfect contrast with the tiny lawns and weedless gardens, the painted tea-houses by the stream, and the frivolously toy-like houses. The inhabitants seemed to him a very successful blend of Chinese and Tibetan; ... they were good-humored and mildly inquisitive, courteous and carefree....

What created the mythic world of "Shangri-La"? Nature's divine workmanship, of course.

The immense geological changes in Yunnan happened at least 1.7 million years ago, when Yuanmou Man, believed to the earliest ancestor of the Chinese, was living in groves and grasslands in Yunnan.

When the ancient seas receded they left behind the amazing 13 peaks of the cloud-

piercing Yulong (Jade Dragon) Snow Mountain above Lijiang. The towering snow peaks and ridges and the Jinsha, Lancang (Mekong) and Nujiang (Salween) rivers that flow between them form countless mysterious plateau lakes as well as the unique phenomenon of the "Three Parallel Rivers."

Between the late 19th and early 20th century, many European explorers and missionaries entered the area by different routes, and explored it for different purposes. Back then the name "Shangri-La" was unknown. The many records of their explorations — in German, French and English — have been preserved for nearly a century in an isolated Catholic church at Cizhong Village in Yunnan's Dechen County, which is

within the area of "Shangri-La" later depicted by Hilton.

These include the records of a French explorer who came to Yunnan in the early 19th century and walked through the Tibetan areas of northwest Yunnan, and drew the earliest route map of the area from Cikaluo to Weixi, marking the villages, mountains, rivers and paths. The map was published in the October 1875 *Bulletin de la Societé de Géographie.*

In the spring of 1895, a French bishop Henri d'Orléans and his team left the Gulf of Tonkin (today's Beibu Gulf) in Vietnam and reached the valleys of the Lancang and Dulong rivers in northwest Yunnan by way of Mengzi in southern Yunnan. They stayed with local ethnic groups, including Yi, Hani, Bai, Lisu, Naxi, Derung and Pumi.

These explorations took place scores of years earlier than *Lost Horizon,* and what they saw were similar to what Hilton described. They witnessed the fascinating scenery, rivers running between towering mountains, verdant grasslands set off by the snow mountains, quiet blue valleys in moonlight, lush magical rainforests, ancient, strange villages and tribes tucked deep in the high mountains, old music and written languages, the mystical dances and customs.... Different religions and folk traditions mingle here, all retaining their original character. For millennia the different groups have lived and multiplied peacefully on this land largely untouched by large-scale wars or killing. The beautiful, miraculous land on the south-

| Church in Cizhong Village

west China plateau has witnessed a rich, brilliant history of harmonious coexistence between local ethnic groups.

The novel is not real, but the "Shangri-La" is. On September 14, 1997 the people's government of Yunnan Province made a stunning announcement that Shangri-La had been found in Dechen Tibetan Autonomous Prefecture, Yunnan Province. The conclusion had been made by groups of natural scientists, anthropologists and geographers after years of investigations, explorations and argumentations. A fairy land well-known to the world became reality in Yunnan.

This is Yunnan, Hilton's "Shangri-La"— source of so much inspiration, aspiration and imagination.

South of the Rosy Clouds

In Shang Dynasty oracle bone inscriptions dating from the 11th century BC, the Yunnan-Guizhou Plateau is referred to a "ghost area." This shows how China's ancestors pictured this mysterious land; to the ancient people of the Central Plains, Yunnan in the remote southwest was a barbarous wilderness. It is said that Emperor Wu (140 BC-87 BC) of the Han Dynasty used to gaze into the south from his palace, and, finding

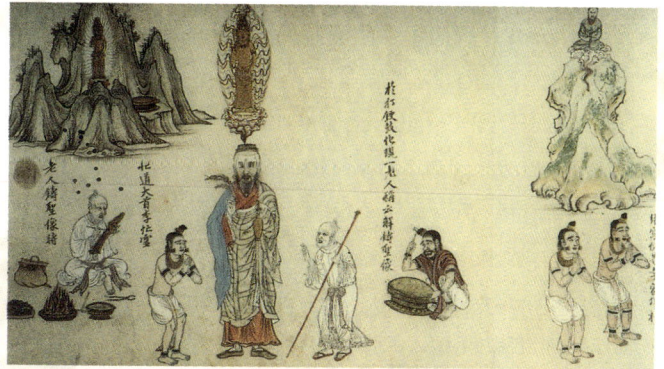

▲ Zhangshengwen scroll painting created in the Dali Kingdom period
▶ Nanzhao scroll painting

that rosy-colored clouds always appeared from this direction, imagined that it must be a fairyland. Encouraged by his ministers, who told him that below these auspicious clouds there lay a precious land waiting to be won by the Han, the ambitious Emperor Wu dispatched more than 100 emissaries between 124 BC and 120 BC to look for it in the south. After two months walking, they arrived at what is now Dali, and decided that this was the place they were looking for, a place of good geomantic auspice that should come under the rule of the Han. Soon afterwards, Emperor Wu established Yunnan (South of the Clouds) County there, which was later re-named Xiangyun (Auspicious Clouds) County. The story of the "rosy clouds rising from the south" was handed down, and "Yunnan" became the name of the province.

The central governments of all dynasties exercised effective rule over Yunnan. In the Sui and Tang dynasties (581-907 A.D.), the Nanzhao Kingdom centering on Erhai Lake was established. The vast territory under its control included today's Yunnan Province and large areas beyond and it represented an important part of the Tang empire. The Nanzhao Kingdom practiced a policy of mutual tolerance between Han and aboriginal cultures, which resulted in the harmonious mingling of Han, Tibetan and aboriginal cultures, thus influencing many aspects of local social life and historical culture in later years.

After the Nanzhao Kingdom was overthrown, the Song Dynasty (960-1279) set up the Dali Kingdom, centered on what is present-day Dali. This kingdom was closer to Han culture and identified with it in more aspects. As a result, Han culture permeated and blended with the cultures of local ethnic groups, giving rise to the development of a more

Excavated articles from the ancient Dian Kingdom, 2000 years ago
- ▲ Gilt container with knight
- ▲ Bronze house
- ▶ Bronze footed vessel with ox and tiger decorations

YUNNAN

Tibetans planting tulips

harmonious, multi-faceted local culture.

Yunnan as a Province was first established in the Yuan Dynasty (1271-1368). Kunming has been the province's administrative center down the centuries.

Central government's development and administration of Yunnan through the ages have drawn the region's multiple ethnic

The Jingpo minority Munao Festival

groups into the fold. Historically isolated from the outside world by its mountains and rivers, Yunnan's local cultures still show a strong vitality. The aboriginal cultures feature pantheistic and polytheistic beliefs, which add mystery and color to this southern, red-soiled land.

Home to Different Ethnic Groups

This mysterious, beautiful land of wondrous natural landscapes and rich natural resources is home to many different ethnic minorities. The ethnic minority population of Yunnan is 14.6 million — one third of the total in the province. Of the 55 ethnic minority groups in China, 51 are represented in Yunnan, and of these, 25 have populations in excess of 5,000 and relatively fixed areas of habitation. Fifteen ethnic minority groups live only in Yunnan, namely, the Bai, Hani, Dai, Lisu, Wa, Lahu, Naxi, Jingpo, Blang, Pumi, Nu, De'ang, Derung, Achang and Jino. They still keep their own distinct cultures but co-exist in harmony. In Yunnan you will encounter the different customs of the individual peoples; in its old towns and villages, surrounded by fascinating natural scenery and strange traditions, you feel like you are walking in a dream, in a land far removed from worldly hustle and bustle — the enchanting land of "Shangri-La."

YUNNAN
云南

Hada from Buddha

For the Tibetan people in Yunnan, religion is indispensable to their lives. The white snow mountains, blue lakes and green grasslands seem to be able to purify the souls of everyone who passes through this place. The spinning of the prayer wheels symbolize the local people's pious hopes and prayers, their pure world of the spirit transcending the mundane. The sunlight over the snow mountain takes on a great religious solemnity; their folk dances, on the other hand are full of the joy of living.

PANORAMIC CHINA

The land of Shangri-La. Forest coverage in Zhongdian is 75%, comparable to that of Finland, with superb, pollution-free air.

YUNNAN

Tibetan village at sunset

Living in Paradise

The Tibetan people are not indigenous to Yunnan; the majority of Tibetans live in neighboring Tibet, Sichuan and Qinghai. Dechen Prefecture is the single Tibetan autonomous prefecture in Yunnan and Tibetans constitute the majority population in Dechen's three counties.

"Shangri-La" lies in Dechen Prefecture. In Tibetan the word "Shangbala" refers to an ideal world described in Buddhist scriptures, a land where people and deities live harmoniously with nature. A derivative of "Shangbala," "Shangri-La" means "sun and moon in the heart." And the original name of the old city of Zhongdian was "city of sun and moon."

Dechen is a land where life is embraced to the full. Its people here — be they pilgrims following the sun and prostrating themselves with every

| Kangba Tibetan

Tibetan horse racing

step, solitary nomad herdsmen, girls singing their hearts out on the sun-bathed wilderness — are filled with a simple vitality, enthusiasm and thirst for life.

Enter any Tibetan home, you will smell the strong aroma of buttered tea, and the physique of the host and the beauty of the hostess, both wearing traditional dress, will win your admiration.

The horse-riding contest on the fifth day of the fifth lunar month gives the men a chance to show off their bravery and daring. The riders' breathtaking performances — standing on one leg, hanging upside down, or picking up a handkerchief whilst riding — attract admiring glances from the young women spectators.

The nomad tents, caravans and remote villages are isolated from the outside world for most of the time, and it is a real joy for the family — for the whole village even — to receive guests. Tibetans are a hospitable people who regard the coming of guests as an auspicious sign, just like the arrival of a phoenix; not to drink his *qingke* wine and buttered tea, not to eat his preserved meat would be a slight to the urgings of one's host.

YUNNAN

Festive Tibetan dancing

    The deep mountains have shaped the nature of Tibetan people, and inspired their songs and dances. They sing and dance at festivals, when they sow their crops, when they harvest them and as a welcome to guests. They grow up steeped in traditional singing and dancing, and everyone is skilled in the arts — to witness them is enchanting.

Soul Pilgrimage

For many people who have been to Dechen, it is a spiritual place, a place where lay people can encounter holiness and find comfort. Under the pure, bright skies of Dechen glistens the sacred Minling and Baimang snow mountains, mystic canyons and the dreamlike Bita Lake. Nine ethnic groups with different religions live in harmony here. The explorer-botanist Joseph Rock once said that it was "a land where immortals lived." But of course this is not really a dream land, no Garden of Eden; the people

Sumtsen Ling Temple in Dechen was built in the early years of the Qing Dynasty, several hundred years ago.

still have to work hard and struggle with Nature to earn a hard-won living.

Where then is the real "Shangril-La," the real "sacred place," of our hearts? Perhaps the Minling Snow Mountain will provide some clues.

Minling Snow Mountain is also known as "Taizi" or "Kawagebo." It is the "Karakal" of James Hilton's novel. It is actually a group of snow-covered peaks in the Nushan Mountain Range in the border areas between Yunnan and Tibet. The term "Minling Snow Mountain" usually refers to the middle part, represented by the highest of its peaks, the 6,740-meter-high Kawagebo Peak.

"Minling" means "medicine mountain" by reason of its famous medicinal herbs that flourish on the mountain. It ranges for some 150 km long and 30-40 km across and has the largest glacier in Yunnan. Sacred to the Tibetan people, the mountain is a place of pilgrimage for Tibetan Buddhists. It is said to be the guardian deity of Jiajuba, a branch of the Nyingma Sect, visible in the clouds to pious pilgrims at Lhasa's Potala Palace in Tibet. Kawagebo, the highest peak, means "white snow mountain" or "god of snow moun-

YUNNAN

tains" in Tibetan. Legend has it that Kawegabo was once an evil spirit that later converted to Buddhism and became a divine general protecting the frontier. Statues of Kawagebo are often seen on Tibetan people's altars. Every year, in late autumn and early winter, pilgrims pour here from other parts of Yunnan, from Tibet, Sichuan, Qinghai, and Gansu.

The Tibetan population adhere to Tibetan Buddhism, in which Nature and life are paramount. The local people regard Minling as sustenance for their souls and as a sacred symbol. By the roadside leading to the mountain and at its foot are countless Mani cairns — mounds of stones carved with the six-word mantra. These stones, together with the prayer flags fluttering in the wind, and the white *hada* silks, are common spiritual symbols among believers.

Shrouded in clouds and fogs, Minling Snow Mountain dominates vast areas — the magnificent landscape of the Three Parallel Rivers and immense expanses of Sichuan and Tibet. The geological changes of millions of years, the millions upon millions of lives which it has witnessed, seem to be made manifest in its icy, solemn brilliance. It has been an object of veneration for generation upon generation of believers.

In the peaceful sunlight and in worship of the majestic snow mountain, you may feel some re-awakening in those parts of your heart that have become numb. Pilgrims ignore passing cars, tractors even,

◀ Wandering the labyrinthine palaces of Sumtsen Ling Temple, the sound of chanting fills the air, with words of life, death and reincarnation.

◀ Tangka painting at Sumtsen Ling Temple

▶ Tibetan on mountain circuit pilgrimage

when walking along the highway. After their arduous journeys — three days or two weeks — their fear of the deity is replaced by contentment and gratitude, and they feel nothing but peace when gazing up at the snow mountain. To them, the sacred light of Buddha has turned everything holy, and they feel the existence and strength of a mind at peace, when the humble is turned noble in their eyes.

Worship of the Minling Snow Mountain continues to this day. By grasping the sacred *hada* thrown by Buddha, the pilgrims seem to find a sense of fellowship with the world of the immortals.

Local people say that you may only worship the sacred mountain but not climb to the top, otherwise it will take offence.

Elderly people clearly remember that "long, long ago" foreign mountaineers fell into crevasses in the snow, never to be found again.

On June 10, 1987 a Japanese mountaineering expedition retreated from Kawagebo after climbing to 4,500 m.

In June 1987 an American team had to turn back at 4,200 m.

In October 1989 a Sino-Japanese expedition failed to climb Kawagebo from the north side.

From November 25, 1990 to January 3, 1991, a Sino-Japanese expedition was blessed with sunny weather in their arduous climb until they were only 270 m from the summit. Then there was a sudden snow storm and they were forced to return to their nearest camp. That night the 17 mountaineers were killed in an avalanche.

On November 12, 1996 a Sino-Japanese-Nepalese expedition challenged Minling again. At 6,250 m, when they were

YUNNAN

Mountain circuit pilgrims

at the point of reaching the summit, a hard wind blew up, forcing them to return quickly.

Even if, as local beliefs would have it, these failures did mean something mysterious we can find no answer in any of the Buddhist scripture. The local people would rather worship Kawagebo — they have no desire to "conquer" it.

Kawagebo Snow Mountain is the "Karakal" of James Hilton's *Lost Horizon*, Hilton described it as the grandest and most beautiful in the world, a perfect cone of ice and snow resembling a child's drawing. Its height, size and distance could not be gauged. The reality of its radiant serenity was scarcely believable.

A Bird's Eye View of the Three Parallel Rivers

In the valley of the Hengduan Mountain Range, which stretches from northwest Yunnan to the south Qinghai-Tibet Plateau, the Nujiang, Lancang and Jinsha rivers flow parallel for a distance of several hundred kilometers, never converging — the shortest distance between the outside two is a mere 66.3 km. The whole area covers 41,000 sq km. Located at the point where East Asia, South Asia and the Qinghai-Tibet Plateau meet, it is representative of rare alpine landforms and their evolution. In 2003 the Three Parallel Rivers area was listed as World Natural Heritage for its diverse landscapes of high, snow-covered mountains, canyons, dangerous shoals, vast forests, snowfields, glacial lakes, beautiful, vast alpine meadows, rare animals and plants, the magnificent White Water Terrace, and distinct local folklore. It is home to 16 ethnic groups with their respective languages, religious and customs.

As the local myth goes, Jinsha, Lancang and Nujiang were the three daughters of Tanggula Mountain.

The three sisters were to be married to the west but the defiant, beautiful eldest sister Jinsha was in love with the Prince of East Sea so the three sisters decided to run to the east. But their brothers the Haba and Yulong mountains blocked their way. Lancang and Nujiang yielded to their brothers and turned course, abandoning their plan to join the East Sea. But the defiant "Miss Jinsha" shook off her brothers by

YUNNAN

The bend in the Jinsha River (Yangtze) at Benzilan

The Salween (Nujiang) River

YUNNAN

As the result of international cooperation, the international Lancang-Mekong River traffic route, extending 1,000 km between Yunnan and countries of Southeast Asia, has taken shape.

turning north, before suddenly swerving east, running into the embrace of Prince of East Sea. This bend of several hundred kilometers is the "First Bend on the Yangtze River," a world wonder in which a major waterway makes a "U-turn."

Running her own chosen course, "Miss Jinsha" changes her name to Yangtze when she reaches Yibin in Sichuan Province, and continues on with great strength and vigor, swollen by many tributaries en route.

Lancang, the second sister, ran southward beyond Chinese territory, changing her name to Mekong. She enters the bosom of South China Sea after passing through Myanmar, Lao, Thailand, Cambodia and Vietnam, gaining the reputation of "the Danube of the East."

Nujiang, the youngest sister, refused to be married far away, and in a rage took a shortcut to neighboring Myanmar, where she is known as Salween, finally entering the Andaman Sea in the Indian Ocean.

The three sisters run side by side in northwest Yunnan through their river gorges, watering the beautiful landscape along the way. A bird's eye view from the top of Kawagebo, which stands in the "Three Parallel Rivers" area, shows a splendid, mysterious dreamland.

Long ago the Nujiang River Canyon was virtually unvisited. At its northern end lies a fertile plain, the home of several ethnic groups with different beliefs and customs; these include: the Nu, Derung and Lisu people with their primitive beliefs; the Tibetans who are devout adherents of Tibetan Buddhism; and tribes that recently converted to Western religions. The Nu people were the first to settle here, retaining their clan system and totems up to the mid-20th century. The Lemo people, a branch of the Bai, migrated here from distant parts four centuries ago. The largest groups of Lisu people are in settlements on both sides of the Nujiang River.

The Derung have perhaps the smallest population of any Chinese ethnic minority — in 1995 their num-

Hutiao Gorge on the Jinsha River is rich in hydro-energy, ranking third in China. In terms of potential energy, it ranks second.

Derung people

bers stood at 5,302. Historically, the Derung was called "tattoo-faced tribe" and even today you can still see some elderly women with tattooed faces, which are the vestiges of their people's ancient beliefs. This group lives by and gets its name from the Dulong River, which originates in Tibet, and runs through Nujiang Prefecture in Yunnan for about 80 km. The Dulong River Canyon extends west from Gongshan County, the narrowest point of the "three parallel rivers." It is even steeper and narrower than the Nujiang River Canyon, and in this dangerous natural environment the Derung people have developed a distinctive lifestyle. They are honest and unworldly. When harvest season comes, they store their grains in unlocked small huts by the fields without worrying about theft. Hunters and farmers will store their food for their return trip in a tree hole or hang it from a tree, just marking it with a stone. Seeing the stone, no passer-by will touch the food, knowing that it belongs to someone.

YUNNAN

Terraced fields beside the Lancang River

The different ethnic groups with their different beliefs have lived together in peace in this remote area for centuries — just like the never-ceasing Nujiang River, carrying forward the mankind's precious spiritual heritage in the long river of history.

For eons the Lancang River has rushed through high mountains and ridges, nurturing millions of people on both banks, and, in recent years, serving as a source of power.

Since the 1980s, the Manwan, Dachaoshan, Xiaowan and Nuozhadu hydropower stations have been built on the Lancang River. The Manwan and Dachaoshan are already in operation each with a generating capacity of over a million kilowatts. Day and

▲ Hydropower station on the Lancang River
◄ Tibetan village in a valley of Jinsha River

night, these stations are generating power for the east of China. Xiaowan Power Station, currently under construction, will have a capacity of 4.2 million kilowatts and a 292m-high dam. When completed (in 2010) it will be Asia's highest hydropower station.

These dams have reshaped the Lancang River. The torrential flows of the past have become quiet artificial lakes embraced by picturesque wooded mountains. Who would associate this with the mountain-piercing, valley-leaping Lancang?

The dazzling Nujiang, Lancang and Jinsha rivers start in the far west and run their parallel courses through the counties of Dechen, Weixi, Shangri-La, Gongshan,

YUNNAN

Fugong, Lushui, Lanping and Lijiang, which constitute the 1.7-million-hectare core of the UN "World Natural Heritage" area. In some places their flows are slow and quiet, bordered by pale willows and dark pines, creating melodious mountain pastorals. Elsewhere they get wild; the canyons reverberate with their furious, roaring waters that can be heard from miles away. The famous Tiger Leaping Gorge shows how violent the Jinsha River can be; here she meets the Haba and Yulong snow mountains, the brothers who tried to block her way, and where, perhaps still bearing this old grudge, she cannot restrain her rage, but breaks furiously against the hard cliffs with bone-shattering power.

The countless pastures in the Three Parallel Rivers area are the three girls' soft carpets. In the warm spring sunshine, the pastures are dotted with small flowers like colorful gems. The herdsmen lead their yaks to a place with water and lush grass, and let them eat at leisure, while they (and perhaps some tourists too) lie on the grass, gazing skyward at the flying eagles and white clouds, and feeling their own life rising to a higher realm. The distant roaring of the Jinsha or Lancang rivers sounds like a solemn melody of life.

The Baimang Snow Mountains are some 90 km long 30-40 km wide, and have an average altitude in excess of 4,000 m. The area is a state-level nature reserve, preserving large tracts of virgin forest. They are home to the famous Yunnan golden haired monkey.

▲ Autumn view of Shudu Lake
◀ Shudu Lake

YUNNAN

Below the snow mountains along their way, that tower like generals in silver and jade armor, the three sisters present their endless tenderness.

On the side of the snow mountains, enclosed by the forests' embrace and decorating the azalea-clad slopes lie many shimmering lakes. A survey records 424 of them, hiding in isolation in the depth of these three river valleys.

Bitahai and Shuduhai are sister lakes near "Shangri-La" County. Here you will find beautiful, limpid waters of intoxicating blueness, bordered by forest and grassland, with yaks and highland horses. In late spring and early summer, the Bitahai Lake is surrounded by banks of azalea flowers. When the petals fall into the lake, the fish will vie to eat them. The mild narcotic in the petals will quickly intoxicate them, but not fatally.

Another Sacred Place

White Water Terrace is located at Baidi. The place of origin of the Dongba religion, Baidi is a small plain lying west of the Jinsha River and south of Tiger Leaping Gorge. It is known as "Bazi" to the Yunnanese. "Baidi" in the Naxi language means a place flowing with springs where green grass grows.

白水台在白地峡谷西端雪山脚下。周围的大山都是一片赭赫色，唯独它通体晶莹、遍体雪白。远看是一座玲珑剔透的玉山，中景是

YUNNAN

In the 1930s, the naturalist Joseph Rock came to this place by mule and the sight took his breath away.

▲ White Water Terrace
◀ Dongba sacrificial ceremony

The slopes are densely covered with pine trees and oaks, under which bloom Photinia flowers in pink, red and white. It is a fairyland spot, its cool, pleasant air full of birdsong.
Dwarfed by the sight of the magnificent landscape with its deep valleys,

PANORAMIC CHINA

snow-covered mountains, huge rocks and lovely forests, you cannot but feel how tiny you are.

The sacred cave of Xiluonike is a well-known place of pilgrimage, as it is the wish of every Naxi shaman to make a pilgrimage to it. The cave in the mountain east of Baidi is also known as "Xiluoya Corner." It is said that Xiluo Duoba, founder of the Dongba religion, once lived in the cave and disseminated its beliefs from here.

The sacred cave recorded by Rock is still a place where the people worship. It is a moderate-sized karst cave with stalactites, pillars and stalagmites. Local myths and religion have invested it with a sacred aura.

The ancestors of the Naxi people developed their primitive religion based on pantheism and totem worship. It is quite amazing that it did not originate in Lijiang, which has the greatest concentration of Naxi people, but at Baidi with a small population of a few hundred.

The White Water Terrace is a snow-white terraced land situated at the foot of a snow mountain at the western end of the Baidi Gorge, standing out from

and set off by the brown mountains around. From the distance one sees a jade-like mountain, a closer look shows that it is a "karst waterfall." An even closer inspection reveals that the terraced land is honeycombed with small holes, like the indentations of pearls poured down from heaven. From the top of the White Water Terrace a spring cascades down, its waters spreading open like a fan at all the different levels. Thus the entire jade-like mountain is covered with shallow water.

According to local legend, the source of the White Water Terrace is milk produced by the "White Water Goddess," and transformed into a stream to save the living creatures in the area. Moreover, the terraces created by her dripping waters also showed them how to open up land. The scientific explanation is that the high calcium carbonate content in the spring water is deposited as white particles, which have ultimately grown into this snow-white "divine mountain." In the middle of the "divine mountain" is a rock formation shaped for all the world like a woman's vulva, and this is worshiped by the local people as a fertility symbol.

On the "Chaobai Water" Festival, which falls on the eighth day of the second lunar month every year, the local Naxi, Tibetan, Yi, Bai and Lisu people gather at Baidi; here, among the blossoming wild flowers that fill the mountains and meadows, they sing and dance in celebration of the harvest.

In ancient times, the Baidi, in the embrace of towering mountains, was covered with lush grass and forest, full of flocks of birds and animal herds. In this isolated environment, the local people created a religion from the primitive worship of "divine things," a reflection of their peaceful life spent within the confines of the canyon.

雲南

Treasure Chest of History

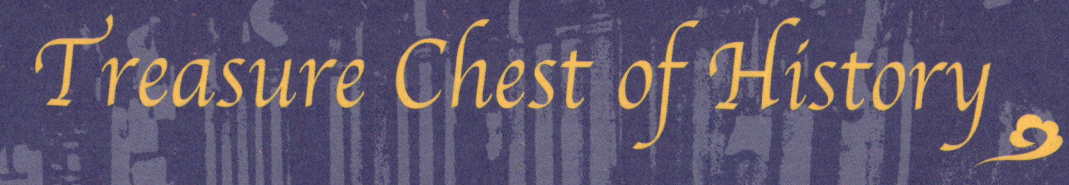

The ancestors of the Naxi people believed that the first human life began when sound and air came together to form dew, and the dewdrops became eggs and the eggs hatched out man. This is a very ancient legend. But in Lijiang, even reality seems ancient. One is compelled to explore with the eye of an archeologist and to think like a historian.

The famous Chinese archeologist Fei Hsiao-tung was deeply attached to Yunnan. Before leaving Yunnan he said, "Yunnan is my second home and I could never forget it. I shall return to Lijiang, return to Yunnan...."

Within the 35 km stretch of the Yulong Snow Mountain are 13 peaks, the highest being 5,596 m, the other 12 all over 5,000 m, and snow-capped all year round. Its flora has been well preserved. Vegetation and views change according to altitude and temperature. Besides spruce, fir, redwood, lily, camellia, primrose and alpine rhododendron, there are medicinal plants such as ginseng, angelica and tuber of elevated gastrodis. Thus, Lijiang has long had the sobriquet "herbal medicine village."

Welcoming
Bosom of the Old Town

Learning about the "antiquity" of Lijiang starts with the newspapers and magazine accounts of this small town that have been published around the world.

YUNNAN

It is known as "Old Town," but its real name — Dayan — is not well-known.

The old town sits on tableland at 2,400 m above sea level under Yulong Snow Mountain in Lijiang Naxi Autonomous County. It has an area of 3.8 sq km. The town has no regular street layout or surrounding walls, and its buildings are arranged in graceful disorder according to the terrain.

The Square Street is the "center" of the Old Town.

▲ Residents washing vegetables and carrying water by a *sanyan* ("three eye") well in Li Jiang's Old Town. The "wells" in the Old Town in fact are fountains bubbling up from underground. Residents built stone or brickwork around the fountain, adapting it for their daily needs. Most of the traditional wells here are *sanyan* wells—i.e. three separate fenced-off sections; the upstream, most pure and pollution-free fountainhead, is used for drinking water; the second has clean water for washing vegetable; the downstream one is for washing clothes.

◀ Naxi homes built by the water
◀ Lijiang Old Town beneath Yulong Snow Mountain

    The town is full of old, simple houses and winding streets. Clear streams zigzag their watery way through the town, passing by practically every house.

    There are no high-rise buildings or noisy discos; you will feel you are walking through the streets of a century past. The refreshing sunlight shines down between the dense moss-covered houses, and the breeze coming from Yulong Snow Mountain outside the town is cool, never cold. The residents of the old town are as gentle and mild as their climate.

    To the people of Lijiang, Yulong Snow Mountain is sacred. For centuries legends about Yulong have been associated with the beginning of the universe and human life. The Naxi people piously believe that it has blessed their numbers, since their ancestors, from the ancient Qiang tribe in northeastern Tibet, migrated there several centuries earlier.

Ski run below Yulong Snow Mountain

Lijiang Old Town was first known as "Gongbenzhi," which in Naxi means "storehouse, village and market." It was built between the late 12th and mid-13th centuries, and governed by a chieftain named Mu — a synonym for wood. Lijiang is the only town in China not to have wall built around it, the reason for this lying in the symbolism of Chinese characters; when you draw a square line (like a town wall) around the character *mu* (wood), the resulting character *kun* is the word for "bondage," something the Mu clan would rather avoid.

The Mufu Palace in Lijiang, residence of the historically famous Naxi Chieftain Mu. The modern version replicates the style of the original Ming Dynasty complex. Chieftain Mu had his palace halls built facing east toward the rising sun, as the East comes under the category of wood (*mu*), according to ancient Chinese theory of the five elements. Mu was also the surname given by the emperor to Naxi chieftains.

The Mufu Palace looks like a king's residence, but unlike other Chinese cities it lies in the south rather than the center. The city center was Sifang Street, from which roads radiated in all directions, attracting many merchants. Clearly old Lijiang began life as a village market, and rose to prosperity from trade and commerce. This had much to do with its being an important town on the "ancient tea and horse road."

In the Ming Dynasty (1368-1644) Chieftain Mu royal buildings were grand enough to make the contemporary traveler and geographer Xu Xiake exclaim "the mansion is as beautiful as a royal palace." In the Ming Dynasty, Lijiang's population numbered over 1,000 households, and residential construction in the city had reached a considerable scale.

Peaceful lives of Old Town dwellers

Decorative windows and couplet in an Old Town dwelling

YUNNAN

And indeed today's unenclosed Old Town is open to the world, old in style but by no means conservative.

The winding, water-lined lanes follow the lie of the land. Walk along their shop-flanked course, and pleasant discoveries lie in wait — perhaps you'll chance upon a gorgeously decorated courtyard, perhaps upon the fragrance of rare flowers.... Now, just as it did in the ancient past, the sunshine pours down as ever onto Lijiang's peaceful modest households and showy establishments alike.

The houses of the Naxi people in the town are either single- or two-storied, with a neat courtyard. Simple in layout, the houses integrate Han, Bai and Tibetan architectural features. The screen walls in the residences bear elegant traditional Chinese ink paintings of orchids, peonies, green pine trees and white cranes. The decorative motifs on the doors and windows include peacocks and pheasants, dragons and phoenixes, golden deer, eagles and other auspicious animals popular with the Chinese.

The old town has many other surprises in store. For example, there are 354 stone bridges over the three streams that thread through this small town. The Bridge of Ten Thousand Sons, built by a childless man in the Ming Dynasty (1368-1644), became his "merit" and brought him many sons and grandsons. The Bridge of Longevity was built during the Qing Dynasty (1644-1911) to commemorate a Lijiang father and son, both of whom lived for over 100 years. The Imperial Band Bridge was built by the chieftain Mu based on the Gold Water Bridge in Beijing's Forbidden City. There are also "Bridge of Chicken and Pea Jelly Vendors" and "Bridge of Duck Egg Vendors." The bridges served as markets as well as crossings for merchant and caravan routes. Today, there are still vendors selling duck eggs, bean jellies, melon seeds and sugarcanes on the bridges, though no vehicles are allowed.

YUNNAN

The openness and tolerance of this old town have long attracted foreign tourists in great number; any visitor, of whatever nationality and speaking whatever language, will find peace of mind. The local residents are mainly Naxi, who are friendly to strangers and willing to share the old town's tranquility with them. Many incomers have decided to settle here too.

The Ancient Tea and Horse Road

Caravan on the ancient tea and horse road

YUNNAN

    The people of Lijiang were among the pioneers of trade, and caravans were the engine of commerce.

    Before the building of highways, the only links that Yunnan's mountain areas had with the outside world consisted of "post road" paths. In times past, for people living locked away in the mountains, their desire for communications with the world outside was realized through mules and horses. A transport industry emerged, where individuals or groups would drive dozens or even a hundred or more horses carrying goods to and fro along the paths. A trip might take anything from a few days to a few months. The caravan drivers were rough and ready, free-wheeling types, robust in both their build and their views. Each caravan was led by a trail-boss and his word was law. When the caravan was on the move, the drivers would strike gongs to alert people and

| Crossing an iron chain bridge

caravans coming from the opposite direction, the drums sounding through the mountains like car horns today, alerting people to "road safety."

Trade reached wherever horses could reach, and wherever they arrived the merchant caravans brought mutual benefit—they brought culture and they brought the desires and temptations of the outside world. By means of caravans Yunnan developed its trade with Tibet and Sichuan in China, Myanmar and India.

Historically, governments also valued this complex of transportation links, and provided support and protection, including improving roads, building post stations and organizing government caravans. There were countless private caravans, too. For centuries, the world-famous "Tea and Horse Road" was trodden by horses carrying tea, medicinal materials, pelts, salt, and gold and silver jewelry from Yunnan to Tibet, India and even Pakistan. During the Second World War, when all overland routes between China and foreign countries were cut off, the Yunnan caravans played a significant role in transportation, with over 8,000 mules and horses and over 20,000 yaks plying this ancient road

Lijiang was a transport hub where caravans passed through and merchants gathered. It is said that the streets of the old town were built wide enough to allow two horses loaded with goods to pass each other.

A Russian named Peter Goullart visited Lijiang in the 1940s, and wrote the book *Forgotten Kingdom: Eight Years in Likiang*. Here he paints a picture of commercial life in the old town:

YUNNAN

The descent from our hill down to the market below was gradual, along a cobbled street with a stone-flagged path in the center. The street was lined by dilapidated shops in which beautiful brass padlocks, in native style, were made; or those of Tibetan boot-makers, and the sellers of food. The mean exteriors concealed handsome, carved living-quarters behind....

The shops were well stocked with all kinds of merchandise. Tibetan caravans were

Mule caravan and foreign tourists

pouring in the goods from Calcutta, both for local consumption and for re-export to Kunming, at a prodigious rate. Best makes of British and American cigarettes were available and all kinds of textiles. Even new Singer sewing-machines could be bought. Of course, the prices were very high as the caravan is the most expensive mode of transport in the world. One shop had a small stock of imported beer at twenty-five dollars a bottle; few could aspire to buy such nectar. Matches cost fifty cents a box

and were used only in emergencies. Some households always had a few live embers left in the stove from the previous day and neighbors would call in the morning to borrow a burning piece of charcoal.

The shops opened towards noon and the market-place began to function only in the afternoon. In the morning both the market-place and streets were deserted....

The shops were run, with very few exceptions, by women.... They were shrewd and aggressive and knew how to clinch a bargain. When the woman had to go away, she asked her husband to take over. He was usually to be found at the back of the shop nursing a child and his emergence was a calamity to the business and a trouble to himself. He did not know where matches were kept or where to find the pickles or in which jar was the required wine....

What he describes is a microcosm of the prosperous commerce in Lijiang over 60 years ago.

Today, the residents of Lijiang are still adept at business; in particular their trade in

Naxi craftsman making a wood carving

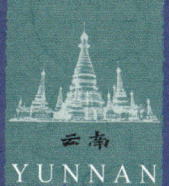

YUNNAN

Caravan going through Lijiang Old Town

traditional handicrafts is better than the past. Along Jinxin Street in the old town are shops selling handicrafts made by artisans from Lijiang or neighboring Heqing, which include bronze locks, gongs, woks and ladles, Bodhisattva statues and old-style vases.

Now the "Tea and Horse Road" is history; the caravans have disappeared and Lijiang has acquired an airport and expressway. The old town remains the same. The new town built alongside it, for all its rivers of traffic and brightly illuminated nights, can never outshine the old town.

Ancient Dongba Culture

　　The seductive scenery of Lijiang attracts streams of people and retains many, but even more beguiling is the ancient Dongba culture. The most singular aspect of this culture is the vehicle for its transmission, namely the Dongba script. Dongba culture is embodied most vividly in Naxi life by a whole series of Dongba religious activities,

　　The pictographic Dongba characters were invented by the Naxi over a thousand years ago. Its name in Naxi language means "mark wood and stone as they are." A classic example of a pictographic script, Dongba today has 1,400 known symbols.

　　After the invention of this script Dongba priests used these pictographic characters to write down the Dongba Scriptures. Today, the ancient Chinese characters that were carved on tortoise shells or animal bones have long disappeared from use, but the Dongba characters are still in use and are called "living fossils." The tens of thousands of Dongba scriptures written with these pictographs

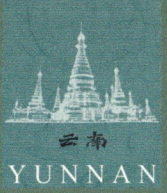

YUNNAN

Dongba totem pictures

are rare treasures and a magnet for international scholars.

The Dongba characters in simple, exaggerated, vivid shapes were drawn in ink made of pine soot and glue, with sharpened bamboo sticks on a kind of locally produced wood-fiber paper. There are thousands of scriptures written in the script, some even painted in colors. The Dongba Scriptures record the Naxi ancestors' meditations on the universe and human life, their searching into heaven, earth, human beings, deities and ghosts, and their simple and philosophical interpretation of the origin of the world.

The Dongba characters have attracted the attention of Western scholars since the mid-19th century. When Joseph Rock visited the White Water

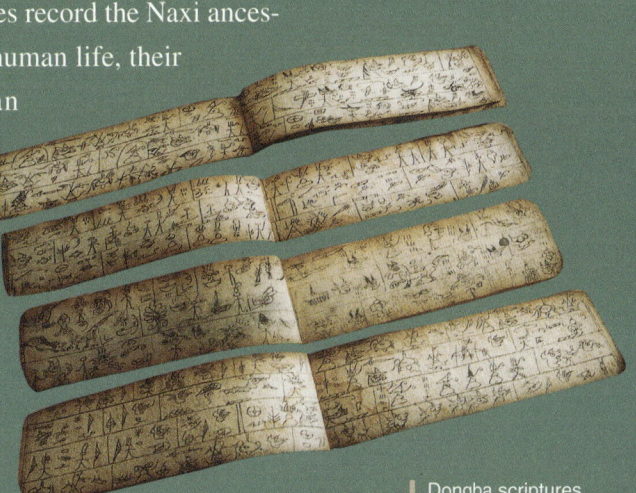

Dongba scriptures

Fabric curtain covered in Dongba hieroglyphs

Terrace, where the Dongba religion originated, he was fascinated by the pictographic characters. He stayed in Lijiang for 28 years, studying Dongba characters at the same time as his botanical research. He wrote more than a dozen books on Dongba characters, and was reputed as the "Father of Naxi Studies."

In recent years, since the opening of China to the outside world, the Old Town of Lijiang has received countless scholars from the United States, the United Kingdom, France, Norway, Denmark, Japan, Canada, Italy and other countries, who have promoted Dongba studies.

The culture has penetrated deep into the Naxi people's bloodstream, a quiet or dynamic force, strongly influencing their thinking and lives, until they end their days. Dongba culture can be compared to an immense pair of arms embracing the Naxi ancestors, the Old Town of Lijiang and the souls of the Naxi people.

The origin and core of the Dongba culture is the Dongba religion. The ancestors of the Naxi people formed their primitive natural religion on a pantheistic basis, and it absorbed some Tibetan Bon and Tibetan Buddhism content. Though the religion originated at Baidi in "Shangri-La" it developed in and spread from Lijiang.

Aming, one of the founders of the religion, disseminated the Dongba religion at Baisha in Lijiang. He standardized the pictographic characters and wrote the Dongba Scriptures. From then on the Naxi people had their own spiritual support, believing that the souls of the dead and the lives of the newborn could all find spiritual sustenance and meaning.

The Naxi Dongba belief system is actually a secularized religion based on pantheism. It holds that deities and human beings are similar in their appearance and ways of living. For example, the heavenly

▲ The Baisha mural, painted during the Ming and Qing dynasties in the Liuli Hall and Dabaoji Palace at Baisha Township in Lijiang, combining Buddhist, Taoist and Lamaist stories in a single picture. It also used Han, Tibetan, Bai and Naxi painting techniques, creating a striking artistic fusion.

◄ Wooden boards incised with Dongba totem pictures

god Zilao Apu is believed to be a shepherd who also hunts with his dog, and catches fish. The Yang god and the Yin god milk cows, husk wheat and weave carpets. The gods live in the same houses as ordinary human beings, and have their own cattle pens, stables, sheepfolds, grain sunning racks and fire pits. Because of the total secularization of their religion, the Naxi people's imaginations of their gods are confined to things relevant to their life. In Dongba doctrine, the other world is depicted as a peaceful pastoral world.

Dongba religion holds that everything has a soul, and its believers worship Nature, their ancestors and life, respecting the harmonious relationship between human beings and Nature. These inclusive beliefs have permeated their everyday life and become standards governing how they behave. The basic principles of Dongba religion are present in Naxi agriculture, husbandry, warfare, astronomy, calendar, literature, art, geography and history. The wide-spread myths, sacrificial rites, ceremonies and living customs have deep influence on the people. Through the power of "Dongba," the Naxi people obtain spiritual consolation in times of confusion, suffering and disaster.

The priests are called "Dongba." They pre-

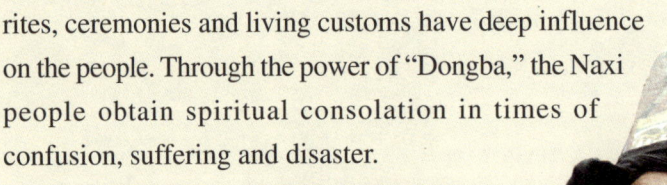

Naxi people's Dongba sacrificial ceremony

side over rites and ceremonies, chant scriptures and are regarded as sages by the Naxi people. With their learning, medical knowledge, multiple skills and sorceries, they have exerted significant influence on the everyday Naxi life for centuries.

There is no Dongba temple, no Dongba "monks," which shows the complete integration of the religion with Naxi secular life. On top of holding sacrificial rites, the priests also farm or do other work, just like lay people.

There are various Dongba rites including offering sacrifices to Heaven (the earliest ancestors and gods), to the god of nature (who is believed to be a half brother of the Naxi first ancestor), to their ancestors (to show the dead the way to heaven), and to lovers who committed suicide (to release their souls). As with the religions of other minorities, Dongba priests demonstrate their communication with deities through sacrificial rites. Surrounded by fluttering flags and incense smoke, by tables covered with

dough animals, Dongba priests, clad in robes of different colors and wearing lotus-shaped hats, brandishing swords, will dance in imitation of various animals, jumping, pouncing and turning, to the clashing of gongs and cymbals. From the primitive, mysterious and solemn atmosphere you cannot but experience the sense of an antique spirit that has never withered, and try to fathom the profound truths of humanity and nature.

A more important rite in Dongba religion is offering sacrifices to "shu." The renowned Chinese anthropologist Fei Xiaotong summarizes it thus: "This old rite expresses the ancient people's worship of nature, and manifests their awareness of 'nature and man in harmony.' This is a major feature of traditional Chinese culture and thinking: that balance, harmony and relationship between man and nature are important; that human beings are a part of nature, not in opposition to it."

The preservation of water sources, forests and vegetation in Lijiang is a result of the Naxi people's respect for and worship of nature. Regarding them as spirits incarnations they instinctively protect every plant. The consciousness of harmonious coexistence with Nature is deep rooted. As children, the Naxi people are told by their elders to protect the natural environment, as the plants and streams around them are spirits that complete their home.

Today, the old Dongba culture is still active in the lives of the Naxi; in particular people still use the Dongba script and it appears on shop signs, calligraphic works, batik clothing, and even on bowls, dishes and tableware.

YUNNAN

Heilong (Black Dragon) Pool and the Yulong (Jade Dragon) Snow Mountain in Lijiang

YUNNAN

Naxi dance

Ancient Naxi Music

Visitors to Lijiang old town will go take in some world-famous ancient Naxi music, either taken by their guide, or by following the strains of the heavenly music they hear by chance when strolling in the evening streets.

The music is played by the Lijiang Dayan Ancient Music Band. In an old quadrangle by a river flanked by green willows, an audience several hundred strong, sits quietly on rows of benches, and on the stage before them sit 20-odd elderly musicians, each playing their own instrument, plucking *pipa* lutes, and three-stringed *sanxian*, playing the two-stringed *huqin*, hitting their gongs and cymbals. In an instant, you feel calmed, transported to another world.

Apart from four young women *pipa* players, the band consists of elderly players in their 70s and 80s, all dressed in long, intricately embroidered

YUNNAN

Performance of ancient Naxi music

gowns. The musicians include a butcher, a trail-boss, a cobbler, a barber, and a photographer.

Naxi ancient music is a kind of Taoist music. Before the performance, the elderly players will pay respects to the God of Literature. This rite is part of the deep-rooted culture.

Taoist music was introduced into Lijiang during the Ming and Qing dynasties. The Ming-dynasty emperor Jiajing (r.1522 - 1566) was a Taoist believer and often had large Taoist bands to play during the rituals of sacrifice to Heaven and Earth. Then Chieftain Mu of Lijiang invited musicians from the capital to teach the music,

so the ancient music is still well preserved in Lijiang, while it has been lost in its place of origin.

The ancient music attracts not only the Chinese people, but also visitors from over 50 countries, including the United States, Britain, France, Germany and Japan. In October 1995, at the invitation of Asian Music Circuit of the Arts Council of England, 10 members of the Dayan Ancient Music Band went to perform in the UK, the first time the band had ever been abroad. The ancient music of Naxi was played by nine elderly men and a 19-year-old woman in famous concert halls, universities and churches across the country.

Later the band went on to Hong Kong, the Netherlands and Norway. At the opening ceremony of the Bergen International Arts Festival, the largest of its kind in northern Europe, the Dayan Ancient Music Band was the only foreign arts group to perform before an audience that included the King of Norway, its Foreign Minister and the Mayor of Bergen.

The band's leading player is Xuan Ke. He is in his 70s but with his lively manner, and square features, you would never guess his true age. The worldwide fame of the band owes much to his eloquence and fluent English.

As a child Xuan Ke was sent by his family to study in a school run by a church in Lijiang, then to Kunming... a music lover since his childhood, he was practically obsessive about the music of his ethnic group — the Naxi. His musical talent has long been widely recognized. The name of this gifted musician is always linked to the ancient music of Naxi and Lijiang.

Rendezvous by Lugu Lake

In the world-creation myths of many countries, it is often women who are the creators of early civilization. It was the sweat and hard work and the maternal instinct of women that shone on the horizon of human civilization. Today those Naxi people (they call themselves Mosuo) living by the Lugu Lake in Ninglang County about 300 km north of Lijiang, still maintain the traditions of a matrilineal society which elsewhere have been lost during the turbulent course of history.

YUNNAN

▲ Young Mosuo couple on Lugu Lake
◄ Mosuo man

To the Mosuo people, love for the mother is even more important than the love between a man and a woman. They respect their mothers and rely on them throughout their lives.

This is a beautiful, free place. The blue water of the Lugu Lake is clear enough to see 40 m under the surface. Small wooden boats drift on the quiet lake, and flocks of wild ducks fly over the water, then land, disturbing the reflections in the lake. The tranquil, green islet in the center of the lake is shrouded in a fine mist. For generations the Mosuo people have lived by this beautiful lake, this land of women protected by Gemu, goddess of its nearby green-clad mountain, enjoying prosperity and freedom.

Mosuo homes are very special. They are built with tiers of thick logs taken from nearby forests, and are known as *muleng* (log cabin) houses. The women's quarters are

Lugu Lake

known as "flower houses," a mystery-shrouded paradise where they enjoy tender loving and delight.

Marriage among the Mosuo people of Lugu Lake is rather unique. The men have secondary status, the position of head of a family being occupied by an elderly woman of the oldest generation. People inherit blood lineage from their mothers. Children live with their mothers, and properties are inherited by women. When it comes to marriage, they never take wives or husbands; instead they have "azhu," or lovers.

It is said that this tradition was created by goddess Gemu, the beautiful, naughty third daughter of Longshen Mountain. The Gods of the Yulong, Jiamu, Guoluo and Zuosuo mountains all proposed to her, but she would rather have "azhu" than being controlled by any of them. Later the people living in the area followed suit. They respect and love the goddess Gemu.

Each day, when the sun sets behind the mountains beyond the Lugu Lake, men set off on horseback or on foot for their lovers' houses, where they spend the night. But they must leave before sunrise. This is the "walking marriage." Men and women can have more than one "azhu" at a time. In the evening, when the man sees a long sword or another man's hat or other belongings hanging on the woman's door, he will go back without making any trouble. Any children a woman has are raised by her brothers, thus uncles enjoy high authority in the family. Even though their mother knows the identity of their natural fathers, her children can only call them uncles.

In this harmonious society by the Lugu Lake, this tradition goes on without interference from the outside world. Even when they break up, the "azhu" do it calmly and find other "azhu." No "azhu" quarrel or fight because of their love affairs.

The Mosuo people have a strong group ethic. To them women are the most reliable, and the harmony and prosperity of the family take priority over anything else. If a woman has many children, her sisters will have fewer children or none at all; and when a woman is entertaining an "azhu" at home, her brothers will stay somewhere else.

In the family, the Mosuo people follow the principle of "uncles preside over rituals and mothers take charge of property." The oldest uncle in the family or a respected

Mosuo people enjoying themselves

male member presides over family sacrificial rituals and association with people outside. The men and women in a family are all equal, and important affairs are decided by the agreement of all the adults. In the family the old uncles, great uncles, mothers and grandmothers are respected, children are well taken care of by the whole family, and the family members live in unity and harmony. Any disabled family member receives special care as a "guardian of the family sent by the Goddess of Mercy."

By the clear lake and green forests, the love of Mosuo men and women floats freely over the breeze-rippled waters, stretching along the moonlit path trodden by the feet of the man walking to his lover's house. From her wooden home drifts a song of "walking marriage."

My love,
Why are you leaving in such a hurry,
When the moon is just over the western mountain?
The fire pit is so warm,
Your lady is so tender.
In a world full of uncertainties we fall in love
And wish our live will last forever.
My love,
I'm filled with sorrow
To know you're going far, far away.

In the square, the young people dance around a bonfire. A young man holds a young woman's hand. Leading him coyly away from the dancing crowd, she thrusts into his hand an embroidered belt, with the words, "Return it to me tomorrow night." It is a hint that she assents to their "walking marriage." Tomorrow night, when the moon rises over the wooden house, there will be a new pair of "azhu."

Ancient Capital at a Crossroads of Asian Culture

In Dali the skies over the Cangshan Mountains stream with unfathomable expanses of rolling clouds and Erhai Lake presents a sight undreamed of. The vaulting skies are wreathed in floating cloud and mist, concealing boundless magic and mystery; below, the earth's misty landscapes, its water-laced fields and pastures, abound with spirit reflections. The closer you get to Dali the more myths you discover, and with them the classic culture of Dali. The writer Han Suyin once asserted that Dali's mythology definitely surpassed that of "The Thousand and One Nights." People have suddenly come to appreciate Dali not just for its beautiful landscapes, but for its culture too.

Cangshan Mountains in Dali

Between Men and Gods

Dali is a place for which men and gods both yearn.

During the Western Han Dynasty (206 BC-24 AD) Dali (known as Yeyu), was the domain of the King of Yeyu. In the Tang Dynasty (618-907) it was the capital of the Nanzhao Kingdom, and of the Dali Kingdom in the Song Dynasty (960-1279).

To the west, the Cangshan Mountains stand like a brocade screen; to the east lies the bright mirror of Erhai Lake.

The Cangshan Mountains contain 19 peaks from north to south, and 18 streams gurgle their way between those 19 heights.

The peaks are snow-capped all year round. Dense towering forests girdle the cloud- and mist-cloaked mountainsides at whose feet lie a patchwork of fields and the green vastness of Erhai Lake.

During the Ming Dynasty (1368-1644), Yang Sheng'an, a former supreme candidate in the imperial examination, was exiled by Emperor Jiajing to do penal servitude in Dali, where he wrote many poems in praise of its scenery. One is selected as below:

◂◂ Erhai Lake is shaped like a human ear. It provides fish, water-routes, electricity and water and is rich in aquatic plants and animals.

In the fifth month Dali's smoky views are special
The whole kingdom free of fretful heat.
By Twin Cranes Bridge people selling snow,
Tasting bowls of snow,
Mixing plums and honey with the snowflakes.

It is said that in ancient times Erhai Lake was a boundless sea and people lived in the mountains. The Goddess of Mercy, Guanyin, who lived in the Cangshan Mountains wanted to borrow half of the lake from its Dragon King, the Rain God, turn it into a plain and give it to the farmers for their crops. The Dragon King demanded that they first build him the colorful jade Wuhua Tower. Under the guidance of Guanyin, the farmers burnt the mountains, smelting rocks from Yunnong Peak in the north to Xieyang Peak in the south and the goddess scattered rosy clouds, flowers, grass, and manna on the rocks. Ninety-nine days later, the mountains were full of colorful rocks with exquisite images of rosy clouds, mist, mountains, and rivers. Today this marble is the renowned "Dali stone." When the tower was completed, the vast waters retreated and fertile land emerged.

The Bai population of this ancient, charming land, naturally have their own myth

about their origins that has been passed down. It is a simple one: when the entire world was flooded, only one man and his sister escaped on a gourd. To carry on humanity, they had no choice but to get married and give birth to later generations.

Of course, historical findings differ from the legend. Three ancient ethic groups — the Dianji, Sou, and Cuan — which assimilated some other groups, were all forebears of the Bai people, a large body of whose ancestors finally settled in Dali.

The area around the Dianchi and Erhai lakes was the birthplace of the earliest culture in southwest China, and cradle of Bai primitive and ancient cultures.

Brilliant myths cover every stone, cave, and leaf in Dali with a veil of unfathomable mystery and magic.

Whether singling the praises of love, retelling tales of courage or promoting justice, the people of Dali use myths and fairytales to encourage virtuous conduct and to wile away their leisure hours.

◀ Erhai Lake

▼ The three pagodas of Chongsheng Temple are the symbol of Dali. The main Qianxun (Thousand Vitarka) Pagoda stands 69.13 m tall, the smaller pair to the north and south are both 42.19 m, the three forming an harmonious whole. The Qianxun Pagoda houses a collection of ancient carvings and scriptures, recording the development of Dali civilization.

Wind, Flowers, Snow, and Moon

*Xiaguan wind, Shangguan flowers, Xiaguan wind caresses Shangguan flowers;
Cangshan snow, Erhai moon, Erhai moon shines on Cangshan snow.*

Wind, flowers, snow and moon are thought of as Dali's four great scenes of nature. Xiaguan, at the source of Erhai Lake, is over 20 km distant from Shangguan, the end of the lake. Wind and flowers link the two extremities. The Xiaguan wind, rough and amorous by turns, whistles around Dali's lakes and mountains at will, whatever the season. Compared with the ruthless typhoon and hurricane, however, the Xiaguan wind inflicts no damage where it passes; it brings eternal springtime to Dali,

YUNNAN

▲ Bai fishermen on Erhai Lake
◄ Cibi Lake

"Island of Immortals," Erhai Lake

then strolls on to Shangguan kissing the camellias, azaleas, orchids, and cactus, surrounded by mountain clouds and mist, or bathed in genial sunshine.

The vast snows that cap Cangshan's lofty and precipitous peaks silently await their assignation with the moon. The moonlight sweeps first across Erhai Lake, sprinkling its surface with silver; then straight off to the mountain peaks, taking their pure white ice and snow in its tight embrace. Every season of the year it repeats this winding circuit.

Naturally such majestic scenery gave rise to many myths. The Xiaguan wind was reputed to be the fierce wind used by a passionate princess, who had been transformed into a white cloud on her death, in an attempt to dry the Erhai Lake so that she could meet her lover, a hunter, who had been transformed into a stone mule and thrown to the bottom of the lake by the abbot of Luoquan Temple. The Shangguan flower was originally a precious pearl transformed into an hibiscus; it belonged to a woodman and his wife who chopped it down when the

YUNNAN

Taihe County magistrate came to appropriate it, after which time the beautiful Shangguan flower disappeared from the earthly world. "The Snows of Cangshan" have to do with a war for defending the homeland; long ago, when enemy troops invaded Dali Kingdom Guanyin sent down heavy snows from the Heavenly Palace, freezing them to death in the Cangshan Mountains. "The Moon of Erhai Lake" tells a morality tale in which evil is condemned and virtue praised; a golden bowl at the bottom of the lake, which had been sunk there by Guanyin in order to quell a black demon dragon doing evil around the lake, turned into a golden moon in the water. A cruel rich man took his whole family to fish for the golden moon, but they all ended up dying in a storm.

In the distant past, Dali's innumerable myths left countless traces in every aspect and every corner of life. The ancient people of Dali used wind, flowers, snow, and moon as sources for tales about matters that closely touched their daily life and that reflected basic aspirations such as security, love, and morality. Appreciating the wind, flowers, snow, and moon as something beautiful to look on, was something for later generations.

| Natural *Taiji* (the ultimate) symbol in Yunlong County

Dali

Dali's long history can be traced back to the Tianbao reign period (742-755) of the Tang Dynasty. Dali's rich accumulation of cultural tradition has exerted a profound influence on all Yunnan and Dali's history accounts for half of the province's history. Known as Nanzhao in ancient times, Dali became the political, economic, and cultural center of the border regions in southwestern China when the Duan clan established the Dali Kingdom in the Later Jin Dynasty (936-947). Xu Xiake, a Ming Dynasty traveler and geographer, devoted a lot of space to

YUNNAN

▲ Bai girl
◀ Dali ancient city gate

Dali in his travel notes. The Venetian traveler Marco Polo, who spent 1275 to 1292 in China, described the sights and sounds of Dali in great detail, exclaiming that its prosperity could match that of Italy.

The name Dali refers both to a specific town and to an administrative prefecture — Dali Bai Autonomous Prefecture which has jurisdiction over 10 counties.

Dali Prefecture is mainly inhabited by the Yi and the Bai ethnic groups, the latter being more numerous. All the Bai people (whose name means white) have a high regard for the color white. In Dali, the men usually wear white front-buttoned jackets and women white jackets and red vests. Older women largely wear blue and white jackets. Unmarried women wear their hair braided and coiled on top of their heads and lace a bright red band around their

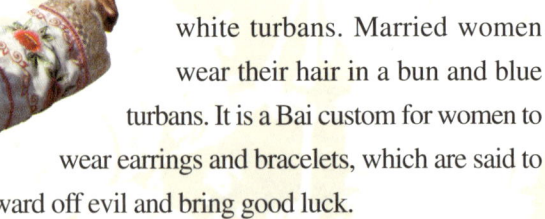

white turbans. Married women wear their hair in a bun and blue turbans. It is a Bai custom for women to wear earrings and bracelets, which are said to ward off evil and bring good luck.

Apart from Buddhism, the Bai people all believe in Benzhu (supreme local guardian deities) and, in Bai-populated areas, almost every village has its own particular Benzhu. Benzhu derives from primitive worship, ancestor worship, and hero worship; the local deities may be a heavenly god, a national hero, a huge rock that once blocked off a flood, or ingenious animal spirits. At the annual Benzhu Festival, people carry their Benzhu statues on colorful sedan chairs, waving banners, beating gongs and drums. Every household burns incense in a censer to welcome their own Benzhu. In this way, the Bai people pray for good yields in their crops, livestock and fisheries and for a happy life.

Benzhu worship is relatively simple and austere, making offerings at a niche in the home containing a deity's statue or picture, simple but elegant. It is evident that the Bai people have an austere understanding of the religious deities of their own nationality.

Bai Domestic Architecture in Dali

Bai domestic architecture in Dali is most distinctive. Its distinguishing feature is "houses on three sides and a screen wall on the other," i.e. a tall main house, two lower wings, and a screen wall opposite the main house, forming a courtyard. The houses commonly feature woodcarving and large quantities of stone are used for decoration. The courtyards are usually quiet and secluded with grass and flowers, carved and painted structure, paintings and calligraphy on the walls, revealing the influence of Chinese traditional arts on this remote people.

YUNNAN

Bai architecture is famous in Yunnan; domestic buildings aside, it boasts a magnificent history in the building of palaces, temples, pagodas and bridges. Records on the architecture of the Nanzhao Kingdom in its heyday show the great contribution of the Bai people.

The Spring Fair

Legend has it that, in the Yonghui years (650-655) in the Tang Dynasty, Guanyin came to Dali and preached Buddhist scriptures in the Bai language. The audience grew larger and larger, giving rise to a market. Later Dali became the key trade hub of southwest China, the market gradually developed into a regular fair with a rich ethnic character. Every year since then, between the 15th and 21st days of the 3rd month of

| Bai girls performing a dragon dance on Sanyue Street

the Chinese lunar calendar, the Bai people of Dali have held the grand Spring Fair, running between the foot of Zhonghe Peak to the end of Yu'er Road. Cattle, medicinal herbs, and daily necessities are transported here from all points for trading. The Bai people also race horses, sing folk songs and perform dragon and folk dances; the Bai women in their splendid traditional costume are especially eyecatching in Dali's brilliant sunshine. In 1991 the fair had official status as a Dali Bai Autonomous Prefecture ethnic festival; it is regarded as one of the grandest ethic minority festivals in Yunnan.

Foreigners' Street

Dali is an ancient capital situated at a crossroads of Asian cultures, its history, culture, and religion all liberal and open to contact with the outside world. At a time when China still thought that their women's tiny bound feet were something to be proud of and regarded foreigners with high noses as monsters, Dali, a remote outpost on the southwestern border, had begun to admit foreigners. It was a more important junction than Kunming on the ancient overland southern Silk Road: the Lingguan Road, starting from Chengdu, and the Wuchi Road from Yibin converged at Dali before continuing as one to the kingdoms of Shan (today's Myanmar) and Shendu (today's India).

YUNNAN

In the Western Han Dynasty, merchants from Shan came via Dali as they transported their jewelry, jade, ivory, kapok fabrics, and other goods to the capital Chang'an, either as tribute to the Emperor or for trade. In the Tang Dynasty, the Nanzhao and Shan had particularly close relations. In the Zhenyuan era (785-804), Yimouxun, King of Nanzhao, invited envoys from Shan to accompany their own envoys to Sichuan; these could be counted as the earliest "foreign guests" officially invited to China. Meanwhile, Indian Buddhism spread along the ancient road and was transmitted into the Nanzhao Kingdom from Shan. The Nanzhao Kingdom practiced Mahayana Buddhism right from the founding of the kingdom. In *A Trip to Dali* the Yuan Dynasty scholar Guo Songnian describes things thus "Buddhism prevails among the people of this Kingdom (Dali), which is near to Tianzhu (India) in the west. Every household, rich or poor, has a family hall for worshipping Buddha. Every person, old or young, continually twists a string of prayer beads in their hand." At that time, Chongsheng Temple in Dali boasted an area of 3500 sq m, 890 rooms, 1,1400 copper statues of Buddha, and some 60 or 70 Buddhist pagodas, including the three at the foot of the Cangshan Mountains that are still preserved today. Dali Buddhist beliefs were often integrated into the locals' primitive folk beliefs.

Dali's present-day accessibility by rail, air, and highway has given rise to Yangren (Foreigners') Street where people from all over the world converge.

In fact, the street was not originally established for foreigners at all.

But foreigners came here in search of 'local' items — local products, cultures and customs, and so a street with all Dali's famous specialties emerged, attracting countless "foreign guests" to linger and browse among its marble items, bandhnu crafts, antiques of the Nanzhao Kingdom period, fish casseroles, Bai cakes, etc. Strolling along this street, Chinese witness the openness of the times, the development of border regions, and communication with people from all over the globe; foreigners experience the flavor of an oriental border town and the warmth of home in a foreign land. In the evening, a breeze from the Erhai Lake blows through the street, a radiant spectacle of Dali-style and western bars and shops full of traditional arts and crafts. Entertained by beautiful female managers who can usually speak a few words of Japanese, English or Russian, foreigners feel happy to linger on the street.

Shibao Mountain

Over 100 km north of Dali stands a mountain known as Shibao. Among its mountain dense forests is the Shizhong Temple, beside which stands a huge rock resembling an immense ancient bell tottering at the edge of a cliff. The surface of the "bell" is covered all over with superb and regular tortoise shell patterns. No one can explain how Nature could produce such an uncanny stone nor its delicate "tortoise shell engravings." Mythological interpretation is the only resort.

Yunnan's earliest grotto sculptures are also to be found in the Shibao Mountain. They were completed by Bai craftsmen of the Nanzhao Kingdom in the 8th century after over 300 years of toil. There are lifelike sculptures of Tathagata Buddha, Kasyapa and Ananda, the eight guardian deities, the slender-waisted Guanyin, and a deity with elephant head and human body. Two of the 16 grottoes have sculptures of human images — one with statues of the family of Geluofeng, Nanzhao's fifth king, and the other,

"Stone bell" in the Shibao Mountain

YUNNAN

Grotto in the Shibao Mountain

A'ang Bai stone carving in the Shibao Mountain

a scene of King Geluofeng discussing state affairs with top officials. Lively scenes representing politics, economy, and daily life in Dali during the Nanzhao period are executed with consummate craftsmanship.

The A'ang Bai stone carving — symbol of the Bai people's most ancient belief — is also reserved in the Shibao Mountain. A'ang means girl in the Bai language, and Bai, the crack from which babies are born, i.e. female genitals. The sculpture, dating back to 1179, is a relic of Bai female phallic worship. Every year pious Bai women come to worship the A'ang Bai sculpture and pray for sons. The presence of female genital sculpture in grottoes dominated by Buddhist and royal images is a very rare occurrence anywhere in the world.

Menghua Town

Menghua Town (today's Weishan County), situated 130 km north of Dali Town, is where Xinuluo, ancestor of the Nanzhao Kingdom, rose to power.

In the Tang Dynasty, six large tribes appeared in the Erhai Lake Wuman area. All of whose chieftains had the title "Zhao" — the equivalent of "King." The Mengshe Zhao, located in the extreme south of the Wuman area, was also known as Nanzhao (Southern Kingdom). In the mid Kaiyuan reign period (713-741) of the Tang Dynasty, with the support of the Tang court, the Nanzhao chief Piluoge united the six tribes and established the Nanzhao Kingdom, and then moved from Menghua to Taihe Town in Dali.

The Nanzhao Kingdom lasted for 247 years and was ruled by 13 kings. At its largest, its territories covered all of today's Yunnan, southern Sichuan, Guizhou, and western Guangxi provinces. It founded its first capital in Kunming.

Weishan's azure sky seems for ever quiet and profound; milky wisps of mist seem always to swathe the mountainside and the plain below in mystery. The shining Yanggua River courses through the plain; side by side together beneath the blue sky run the modern highway and ancient post road, and from the post road, as if from remote antiquity, ring the low, slow melodies of cowbells .

Weishan County seat is composed of many old straight streets intersecting in a rectangular grid, all set off by luxuriant trees. The streets are not wide, but they are neat, and lined with stores of near-uniform size to form a harmonious streetscape. The lichen growth of years covers the bright gray rooftiles. Every household has flowers and plants on their windowsills upstairs. Below the eaves of some houses hang golden corn cobs or nuts whose name you can't identify. People of various ethnic groups — Han, Bai, Hui, and so on — walk its streets, the men usually wearing wool-lined sheepskin jackets, the women in coarse cloth bluc and white bandhnu dresses.

At the center of Weishan stands the Xinggong Tower, a majestic building more than 600 years old. Inscriptions on the horizontal dark gilded boards at the south and north sides of the Gongchen Tower (Weishan's north gate tower) read, respectively, "Heading the Six Tribes" and "Looking far into the Sky." Viewed from the Gongchen Tower, the whole Weishan plain is as beautiful as a dream.

To the north of Weishan County Town, Weibao Mountain rises like a green lion sitting on its heels. It is said that Xinuluo, ancestor of the Zhao of Mengshe, once cultivated land and rose to power right on Weibao

◂ Xinggong Tower

![Temple buildings on Weibao Mountain]

| Temple buildings on Weibao Mountain

and who is to say he hasn't left his footprints on these old mountain roads? Weibao Mountain is also famous for Taoism. It is recorded that Buddhists and Taoists tussled over the mountain in the past; it now has both Buddhist and Taoist temples. Between the first and 15th day of the second month of the Chinese lunar calendar people of various nationalities — from Weishan, Dali, Eryuan, Midu, and elsewhere — come as pilgrims to the temples here, wearing their own national dress. In every temple the Buddhist abbot or Taoist priest can retell the history and legends of Nanzhao, transporting you from reality to faraway antiquity, and into the realm of ghosts and myths.

Grand Canyon of the Orient

Here Nature's primitive and violent power forces, casting aside all pretence of gentility, have brought forth a furious and turbulent river – the Nujiang. Between the towering peaks of the Gaoligong and Nushan mountains the Nujiang has gouged out the 310 km long Nujiang Grand Canyon, at an average depth of 2500 m and width of 100 m. The government of Nujiang Lisu Autonomous Prefecture and the three counties under its jurisdiction are all squeezed into this unique canyon, referred by some as "the canyon of demons."

Great Valley of the Nujiang (Salween) River

Dauntless People

In this huge gorge, wedged between two high mountains, no matter how close you stand, the loudest shout is inaudible, drowned by the earthshaking billows of the Nujiang River. Run or walk, a few hundred m takes for ever, progress obstructed by sheer abrupt cliffs along the way. Since ancient times the Nujiang River has had no roads. No cowards either.

This is a place for men of indomitable spirit — precisely what the people living around the Nujiang River are all about. Take a ledge — perched over the Nujiang River as high as a 10-story building, with a score or so corn plants growing in its stony fissures. The frail plants shiver in the strong wind from the gorge. Outsiders can never make out how these plants have been grown in such an isolated place with unscalable cliffs above surging waters and a sheer, 20 m rockface between the tiny cornfield and the cliff top. This "cornfield" harvest will bring in less than five yuan ($ 0.6). Nevertheless, the Nujiang River Canyon is full of this

▲ People in the Nujiang River area like *chu* wine; they cannot sing without it! When they've sung themselves to a state of happiness, they drink a *tongxin* "fellow-feeling" cup, cheek-to-cheek, without spilling a drop. Do this and you never forget your drinking partner.
◂ Older woman of the Nu minority

kind of "field," a reflection of its people's admirable indomitability, and of the pitiful hardships of their life.

In the canyon, people of many ethnic groups, such as Lisu, Nu, Tibetan, Bai, Naxi, Derung, Pumi, and Han, procreate and live in harmony. For thousands of years, they have clung tenaciously to their own lifestyles and customs down to the present day.

Generation after generation has worked in cultivation, hunting, and stockbreeding, experiencing the hardships of sowing and joys of harvest, their companions the roaring Nujiang and Dulong rivers, the boundless Gaoligong Mountain, and solemn Biluo Snow Mountain. But they let their hair down at festivals of every kind, festivals such as — the Nu people's Mountain Forest Worshiping Festival on the 4th day of the lunar new year; the Pumi people's Mountain Circumambulating Festival on the 5th day of the 5th lunar month; the Lisu people's Harvest Festival between the 9th and 10th lunar months; and the Nu people's New Year, the Kuoshi Festival (the Lisu New Year), and Derung Kaquewa Festival (the Derung New Year), all in the 12th lunar month. The peoples of the canyon labor all year round — but they have occasion for revelry in every season too.

Braves of Blades and Fire

The Nujiang River region contains the largest concentration of Lisu people. Between the 14th century and 17th centuries, the Lisu crossed the Biluo Snow Mountain into the Nujiang River region. They are agile and intrepid; a knife at the left waist, a bag of arrows at the right, and a crossbow on the right shoulder are standard dress for Lisu men, as well as symbols of their courage and industriousness. Lisu women play an important role in home affairs.

At the Kuoshi Festival (the Lisu New Year) the performance of "climbing the knife mountain" and "crossing the sea of fire" is mesmeric and breathtaking. A 10 meter-high ladder is formed of two bamboo poles, the 42 or 72 rungs made, not of wood, but of sharp blades. The performer — barefoot — steps on the blades and climbs to the top of the ladder as nonchalantly as if he he'd just taken a walk on solid ground. But the audience is in a cold sweat, its heart in its mouth. Suddenly, from above comes the explosion of firecrackers; colored ribbons and snowwhite Lisu rice cakes descend, thrown down as gifts to the audience from atop the blade mountains.

Before climbing the knife mountain, the performer has to go through a sea of fire — another Lisu test of willpower.

Red-hot charcoal is spread on the ground, from which arises broiling heat. The performer first scoops up a handful of the burning coals and rubs them swiftly against his face. He then goes barefoot through the flames, smoke arising from the soles of his feet, sweat rolling down his face and vaporizing as it hits the fire. The performer suddenly lies down and rolls through the flames. Cries of fear burst out among the audience.

YUNNAN

At the end of the 19th century, when British colonialists broke into Pianma Town at the west side of the Gaoligong Mountain, Lisu, Jingpo, Han, and Hui peoples in the Nujiang River area fought the invaders of their own accord for 20 years. Boasting only crossbows and swords, they repelled every attack from an enemy armed with guns and cannons. They fought for their own ethnic group and for the whole nation; praise and reward from the inept Qing Government was not their motivation.

The annual Harvest Festival gives laborers a chance to let rip. After toiling all year in cultivation, herding, hunting and so on, during the festival farm workers can revel in song, dance, and wine. Young men carry bamboo barrels of wine on their backs. Just like the Nujiang River needs a level river bend to slow down its steps after surging over the rapids, these hardworking people need the Harvest Festival (also known as the Wine Month), as relief from their hard grind. The torrential waters of the Nujiang River cannot stop lovers hankering after each other and girls on the opposite bank "slide" over via suspension cable. The suspension cable was once an indispensable means of transport in the daily life of people living along the Nujiang River. These amazing suspension cables could transport cattle as well as people, enabling the hardworking girls to enjoy the festival and graze their cattle at the same time.

Since the 1960s, wide asphalt roads have been constructed in the Nujiang River region and even the snow-bound Dulong River region is accessible by car. A steel suspension bridge now spans the Nujiang River and the suspension cable, which has gradually fallen out of use, has become a historical relic for sightseers.

◄ Lisu men "Climbing the Knife Mountain"
◄ The Lisu minority Kuoshi Festival
▼ Lisu minority crossbow contest

Bathing in Natural Hot Springs

In spring, constantly changing white clouds sail across the azure sky above the Nujiang River. The mountainsides are spread with dazzling white tung flowers and gorgeous pink azaleas; clusters of tenacious wildflowers pop up, even from tiny crevices up on the precipices.

The region abounds with natural hot springs. From the 2nd to 6th days of the lunar new year, Lisu families go to bathe in the hot springs, taking with them lavish food supplies. The very steamy and slightly sulfurous-smelling hot springs, can not only dispel fatigue

Lisu minority "Spring Bath." There are 706 hot springs in 124 of Yunnan's counties, many of them in the Nujiang River canyon.

and limber up the body, but also ward off sickness and misfortune.

If a hot spring is by the side of the river, the young people dig a big sand pit with their hands to "bury" their lovers. The "unlucky" one will be dragged into the pit to be "buried" with layer after layer of fine sand, layer after layer of love. The girls first pretend to cry for a bit, bidding farewell to the "dead." Then they burst into loud laughter, welcoming the new life and future.

After the "burials" they go to bathe in the hot spring, first the elderly and the young people later, men and women bathing together at ease in the same spring. The warm waters of the rippling spring, the smooth-skinned women, the tough-skinned men, and their sweet singing are all rejoicing in this blissful atmosphere. The canyon hot springs have created and conserved a very fine human species.

Sent by God

Christianity originated in Palestine in the 1st century AD. From the 19th century on, Western missionaries began to enter northwest Yunnan from Tibet and Myanmar. Annet Genestier, a French Catholic missionary, was the first Western missionary in the Nujiang River Gorge. In 1897, he and another priest climbed over the Biluo Snow Mountain and came to the picturesque town of Bingzhongluo on the Nujiang River where he built the Baihanluo Church and started missionary work.

The free medical treatment and free instruction in reading and writing, not to mention foreign gramophone music, gradually led to wide acceptance of Christian doctrines and a large numbers of local people became Catholics. In 1930, the

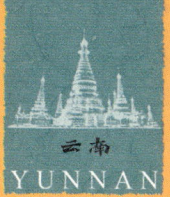

YUNNAN

- Church in the valley
- Church by the Nujiang River

Morse family from America introduced Protestant Christianity to Bingzhongluo. Local religions, such as Lamaism and primitive religion, had to acquiesce in the existence of Western preachers because of the Qing government's support of foreign missionaries. Each religion went about its own business.

Between the 1920s and 1940s, France, Britain, the US, Germany, Switzerland, Canada, and other countries sent altogether more than 100 missionaries to Gongshan, Fugong, Lushui, and other places in the Nujiang River region. James O. Fraser, a British missionary, collaborated with young Lisu teachers in creating a romanized script for the Lisu language, which is still in use today. Missionaries brought Western culture, science and technology to the ethnic minorities in the Yunnan border regions and introduced the folk cultures and customs of these regions back to the West.

Today the number of Christians in the Nujiang River region is around 80,000. Crosses on church spires (statistics say there are over 400 of them), can be seen everywhere in these lofty mountains. The local primitive religion of Benzhu, Buddhism, Taoism, and Lamaism all enjoy equal rights and status with Christianity. In remote villages some old people, taught by missionaries in the past, can read musical notation, even though they are illiterate. In Lushui County, over 100 local peasants formed a chorus to sing a Lisu folk song named Baishi without the guidance of any expert. Their four-part chorus, sung in their untrained voices, was a sensation and hailed as the sounds of nature by experts. The basis for this was their church choir experience.

Lisu chorus

The Peacocks of Freedom

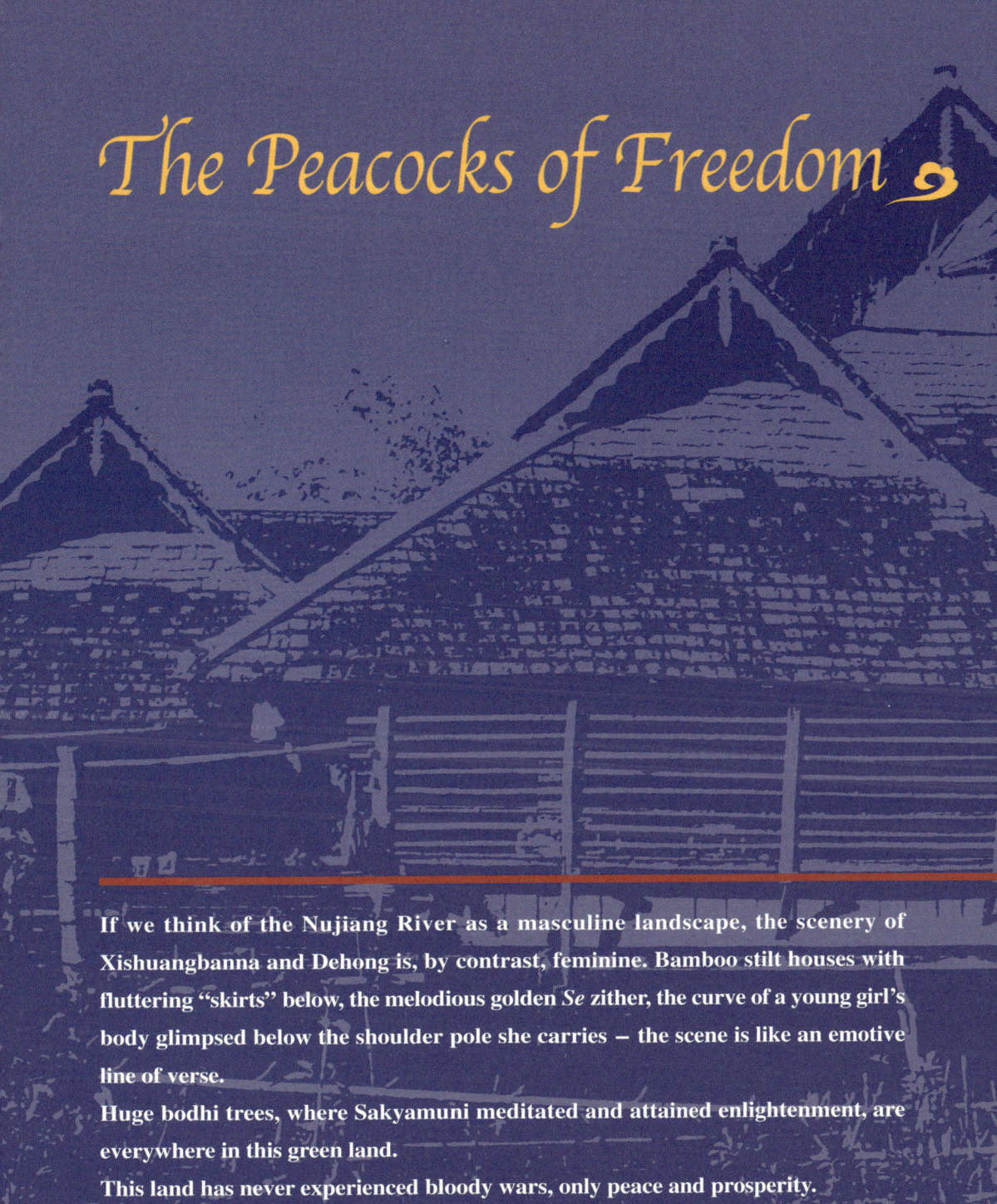

If we think of the Nujiang River as a masculine landscape, the scenery of Xishuangbanna and Dehong is, by contrast, feminine. Bamboo stilt houses with fluttering "skirts" below, the melodious golden *Se* zither, the curve of a young girl's body glimpsed below the shoulder pole she carries — the scene is like an emotive line of verse.

Huge bodhi trees, where Sakyamuni meditated and attained enlightenment, are everywhere in this green land.

This land has never experienced bloody wars, only peace and prosperity.

Last Words at Yunmen

Long ago, the ancestors of the Dai ethnic group lived in northwest Yunnan around the convergence of three rivers. Later, because their population had grown and their living environment had deteriorated, the tribe leaders all decided to lead their people south in search of new homeland where they could live.

Having gone through all manner of hardships, they finally came to a temperate, fertile plain, and built the first town in the history of the Dai people — Yunmen. It has been home to generation after generation of Dai ever since.

It is said that when the chief leader of Yunmen was on his deathbed, fearing that later generations would not draw lessons from their predecessors, he called on all the clansmen and said to them: "I have no wealth to leave you once I am dead, but I do have some words for you that are more precious than any treasures:

◀◀ Morning on the Ruili River

◀ Dense forests provide wildlife ideal habitats. There are 429 identified bird species now in Xishuangbanna, 2/3 of all the species in China and 67 kinds of beasts, 16% of all Chinese species. Some are world or national first rank protected species.
The ancient Dai name for the Lancang River meant "river valley where hundreds of thousands of elephants multiply." The Dai revere elephants as the most intelligent of animals, symbolizing peace and justice.

▶ There are over 20,000 plant species in Xishuangbanna, of which 5,000 are tropical plants and 10,000 edible. Many are rare medicinal plants or have special uses.

▲ Floating along the Luosuo River in Xishuangbanna
▶ Royal water lily

YUNNAN

Living in this world, only if there are good forests can we keep the water sources;
Only if we protect the water sources, can we have
Our hamlets filled with cultivated lands and the plain covered by fields;
Only if we work hard in the fields, can we have
Our barns filled up with grain and folds packed with domestic animals;
Only if we fill our barns with grains and pack the folds with domestic animals,
Can we Dai people survive."

This Yunmen legacy became a life creed for the Dai people. Over the next several thousand years, they continued to move south and exploited the vast green land of tropical rainforest, to establish the homeland of their dreams. Their descendents always bear their ancestors' teaching in mind; to their thinking, a one-hundred-year-old tree is the manifestation or the home of a tree god. Nearby every hamlet, there are always forests dedicated to the gods of the hamlet and the *meng* (former administrative district in Xishuangbanna, Yunnan Province), where people worship and offer sacrifices and where tree felling is a sacrilege. For hundreds of years, the Dai people have cherished the forests and water sources like they cherish their own lives.

The Peacocks of Freedom

The word "Dai" means freedom according to Dai elders. A long time ago, it is said, on the plain where the Dai people lived there were two demons that inflicted adversities without number upon the population. One day, out from the dense, luxuriant forest flew a golden peacock. Displaying its beautiful tail fan, the peacock seduced the two demons to race after it, luring them into an inextricable swamp where they sank deeper and deeper into the mire. That peacock brought the Dai people peace and happiness, so ever since then, the Dai have regarded peacocks as the most beautiful, and most kind of all birds and as a symbol of good luck and happiness. In their eyes, the places favored by golden peacocks are the most suitable for humans. For these reasons, the Dai are extremely fond of peacock imagery and many Dai families rear the birds.

It is also said that the concept of the gorgeous costume worn by young Dai women also originated with peacocks. The story goes that at the time when humankind had just emerged, the concept of clothes did not exist.

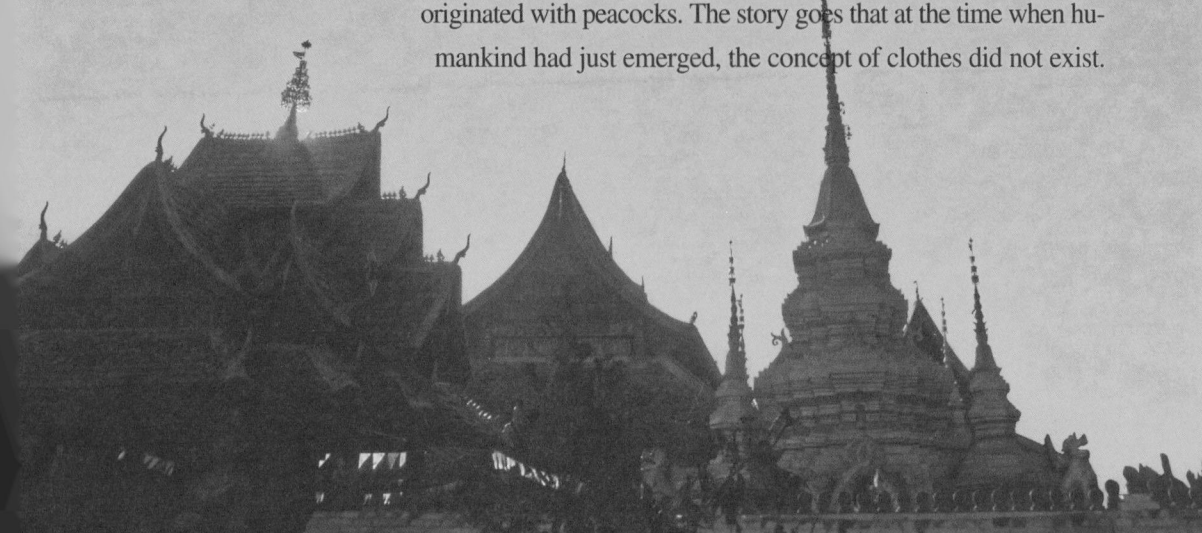

YUNNAN

Jinghong means "city of daybreak" in the Dai language. The legend goes that when Sakyamuni was in Xishuangbanna seeking converts to Buddhism, he walked along the Lancang River all night without seeing a soul, but at dawn finally came across a beautiful plain with flocks of peacocks. So he named the spot "Jinghong."

One springtime, a group of naked girls searching for wild fruits suddenly came across a peacock displaying its tailfeathers; it came to them that if even birds had beautiful feathers to cover their bodies, of course humans too should dress themselves. Thereupon the girls picked banana leaves, wild flowers, pheasant and peacock feathers to fashion themselves rainbow-colored skirts.

In Hinayana Buddhism, which the Dai follow, the peacock is believed to be an auspicious bird, one that takes on and fights monsters and demons and saves living beings; it is considered a sacred bird—an incarnation of the Buddha. Buddhist monasteries are decorated with all sorts of carved peacocks and these are the object of people's devout worship.

In the Jingpo ethnic minority's world-creation epic *Leba Zhaiwa*, the peacock is king of all

the birds. The ancestors of the Jingpo people learned to revere their chief leader from the story "all birds worship the peacock."

Enter a Dai village and you see peacock imagery everywhere: on roofs, clothes, handkerchiefs, doors and windows, even on bamboo hats. The cities of Ruili and Manshi both use the peacock as their emblem. On top of all this the Dai people created the graceful peacock dance.

The peacock dance is the Dai minority's best-known folk dance and many Dai people can perform it well. The process of transmitting the dance down through the generations combined with the creativity of folk artists has resulted in different schools of peacock dance with different characteristics.

The dance content mainly shows peacock movements — scurrying downhill, plodding through the woods, drinking at a spring and playing in its waters, tail displays and flying. Most of the movements are performed in a semi-squatting position, with each joint of the body and arms curved. The dance is rich in movements and postures, particularly hand movements. Varying the shape and movement of the hands whilst retaining the same body posture and stance produces different aesthetic effects and concepts. The dance has strict stylized movements, requirements on positioning, and standard steps, each movement accompanied by drums.

The peacock dance is not only the main source of entertainment for the Dai people, but is also used in Buddhist rituals and at festivals.

YUNNAN

▲ Dai girl

◄ Huayao Dai—a branch of the Dai ethnic group

Dynamic Yunnan

YUNNAN

Yang Liping, a Bai minority dancer and choreographer, was born in Dali Bai Autonomous Prefecture. Her performance of the Peacock Dance is very popular in China, and her dancing has made many feel well disposed toward the Dai people and to Xishuangbanna.

The song and dance drama *Dynamic Yunnan* directed by Yang Liping, displays Yunnan minority peoples' reverence for nature and their love of life. 70% of the troupe comes from minority villages in Yunnan. They have dance in their bloodstream; when Yang Liping recruited them, they were still doing farm work, but in rehearsals, all she needed to teach them was how to use the stage.

"This is the most beautiful dance I have ever seen. I hope she can perform all over the world to let more people know about mysterious Yunnan."
— Mr. Angel Orbetsov, Bulgarian Ambassador to China, after watching *Dynamic Yunnan*

"After today's excellent performance I hope I can go to Yunnan to experience its customs and traditions." — The Cameroonian Ambassador to China

"China and the whole world should share these Yunnan treasures." — The Sri Lankan Ambassador Mr. Nihal Rodrigo

"And then there're the songs, so beautiful, and all original. Yunnan is so attractive." — a teacher

"I have never been to Yunnan, but I feel really drawn to it. I happened to catch *Dynamic Yunnan* in Beijing and think people interested in minority cultures, traditions and arts will hanker after going there once they've seen this show." — a civil servant

"We are moved. Yang Liping's so beautiful. Yunnan's so beautiful." — a courting couple

"I already knew Yang Liping and now I know *Dynamic Yunnan*. Chinese arts are so excellent." — a French girl

One Hamlet Two Countries

There is a beautiful place,
Where the Dai people live,
Each hamlet closely connecting with the next,
The crooked river,
Rippling gently...

YUNNAN

This is a beautiful, appealing song popular all over China. It describes the place the Dai people live as a fairyland — with rain so plentiful it can even turn dry hay green, land so very fertile that planted chopsticks can sprout.

When snow covers the Minling Mountain, flowers are in full blossom along the rivers of Xishuangbanna and Ruili. Intoxicating, eye-dazzling tropical scenery can be enjoyed in every season.

Dai bamboo stilt houses seem to pop up like mushrooms nourished by sunshine and water. Within the bamboo fence surrounding the hamlet are different households blazing with color, coconut trees,

The 4,060-km-long Yunnan border adjoins Burma, Laos and Vietnam. 16 ethnic minorities live on both sides of the boundary line.

fernleaf hedge bamboos, gardenias (michelia champaca), evening primrose...accompanied by the mildly fragrant smell of dirt, shaping the mild and pleasant Dai personality.

Beautiful hamlets with beautiful households are scattered like pearls along Yunnan's borders with Myanmar, Laos and Vietnam. Some such hamlets are divided between two countries but the fact of different nationalities and jurisdictions can't prevent the people-to-people intimacy. People may have different nationalities, but chickens, ducks, flowers and vines do not: It is very common to see Chinese vines climbing abroad to fruit and foreign chickens and ducks laying their eggs in China. If people on "this side" run out of salt when they are cooking, they can just stroll over the border and borrow some from their neighbors on "that side," and get back before the dish is ready.

This happens not just in Dai hamlets; there are altogether 16 ethnic groups living along the borders. Several years ago, when China and Laos defined their boundaries, the boundary line went through a Miao family's house; it was their decision which

Scenes from Dai life
Spinning yarn and weaving cloth
Making paper
Fishing and collecting rubber

YUNNAN

nationality they wanted to be and because the owner's head was in Chinese territory when he slept, the whole family decided to be citizens of China.

This living contact brings with it the exchange of cultures, songs, myths and epic poetry, all of them spreading between peoples on such occasions as weddings, funerals, planting, harvest, hunting, and building houses. Stories such as Zhao Shutun and Princess Peacock and Tale of the Water-Splashing Festival and some Dai folksongs with Buddhist influence enjoy widely popularity in Myanmar, Thailand, Laos and even the Philippines.

Cross-border trade flourishes, increasing day by day. From salt, peanuts, batteries, soaps, and daily necessities to jewelry, jade, timber, home appliances and construction materials — you can see everything traded here. Wherever there is a port or a market, roads on both sides of the frontier are extending, so cars are on the increase and buildings are getting bigger. Ruili, Wanding, Daluo, Mohan, Hekou are all famous Chinese ports. The Lancang River-Mekong River basin is a "golden" tourism route. Water, land and air communication lines connect Xishuangbanna with the Golden Triangle and the Mekong River. Xishuangbanna in China, Luang Prabang in Laos, Chiang Mai and Chiang Rai in Thailand, and Kengtung and Tachilek in Myanmar are all gradually becoming "international parks" on the borders of these four countries.

Morning in the borders is always broken by crows and the barking of dogs which wake up the citizens of two nations. "Cock-a-doodle-doo!" We don't know whether those roosters are under China's fern-leaf hedge bamboos or on the balconies of foreign bamboo houses. It's not important. What is important is the peace, safety and well-being of citizens living along the borders.

Blessing of the Sacred Water

The Dai have lived near water since antiquity. They are a "water" people. From the chief leader's last words at Yunmen we know that they always believed water to be the first principle of the world, and that to protect forests is the only way to conserve water. Consequently, their religious beliefs have given rise to many forms of water worship.

Every mid-April is the Dai Water-splashing Festival, a time when happiness and joy takes over villages large and small. It is known as the "Carnival" of the Orient.

It is said that the Water-splashing Festival is the "Bathing Buddha Festival" or "Buddha's Birthday Festival." It is said that Buddha was born on the 15th day of the sixth month of the Buddhist calendar (mid-April) and that there was a dragon sprinkling fragrant rain to bathe him. Therefore, Buddhists always sprinkle statues of Buddha with fragrant water on Buddha's birthday, and this is probably the origin of the Water-splashing Festival. For the Dai people, water poured on that day is sacred water, water of benediction. On this festival, you can't reject water poured on you because you can't reject auspice and blessing presented to you.

In April, every Dai bamboo home is a hive of activity brewing rice wine, husking rice, making bamboo rockets, butchering pigs in a rush of preparation for the festival. In the fields and at the margins, golden, fragrant "water-splashing flowers" are in full bloom under the scorching sun. They got this lovely name because they bloom at the time of the Water-splash-

Dragon boat race, part of the Dai Water-splashing Festival
Dai Water-splashing Festival

ing Festival. Women pick them to wear in their hair; their long-lasting fragrance is as strong as that of osmanthus. With the start of the Water-splashing Festival, everybody, irrespective of ethnic group, drops their work and celebrates for three to five days.

Generally speaking, the opening ceremony is decorous. Usually, to the accompaniment of beautiful folk song, young girls in pretty, straight skirts hold peacock feathers or fragrant pine branches, dip them into the "golden bowls" full of clear spring water and then gently splash the water onto the head or back of the neck of the elders and honored guests to express courtesy and blessing. Those being splashed accept the blessing with their palms closed together.

Formalities over, people begin to pour water on each other. The water containers have changed from bowls to basins and buckets — a happy water fight begins. On both sides of the street, the government has installed taps at regular intervals so people can get water at will.

Friend or stranger, if you go out of the door you will have water poured over you from who knows where. The more you get splashed, the more blessing you'll have and the more happiness will come your way. And young ladies are always the priority of "blessing."

Regarding the origins of the festival, the Dai people have a tale of 12 beautiful Dai girls who, in ancient times, were abducted by a cruel devil to be his wives. The youngest girl found out when he was happy that the way to kill him was to strangle him with his own hair. However, the devil's head started to flame up and burn, so, in order not to bring disaster upon the earth, the 12 girls took turns in holding it tight and pouring water onto it. Moved by this, people also started pouring water one by one. They finally succeeded in dousing the flames and rinsed the girls' bodies clean with clear spring water. From then on, the Dai people fixed that day as the Water-splashing Festival.

At the festival, people also play with *"gaosheng,"* gunpowder-propelled bamboo rockets set off from a high ladder-like rack.

Dragonboat racing is another important festival activity. To the sound of fast, low drumbeats, racers race their dragonboats. The most beguiling thing perhaps is the women's dragonboat team, composed of Dai girls in red or yellow tube skirts.

YUNNAN

Firing *"gaosheng"* bamboo rockets at the Water-splashing Festival

Religion Between Priestly and Secular

All Dai society adheres to Hinayana Buddhism, perhaps influenced by the changes throughout their history and their special geographical environment. Hinayana Buddhism originated in ancient India and was introduced into Xishuangbanna via Sri Lanka, Thailand and

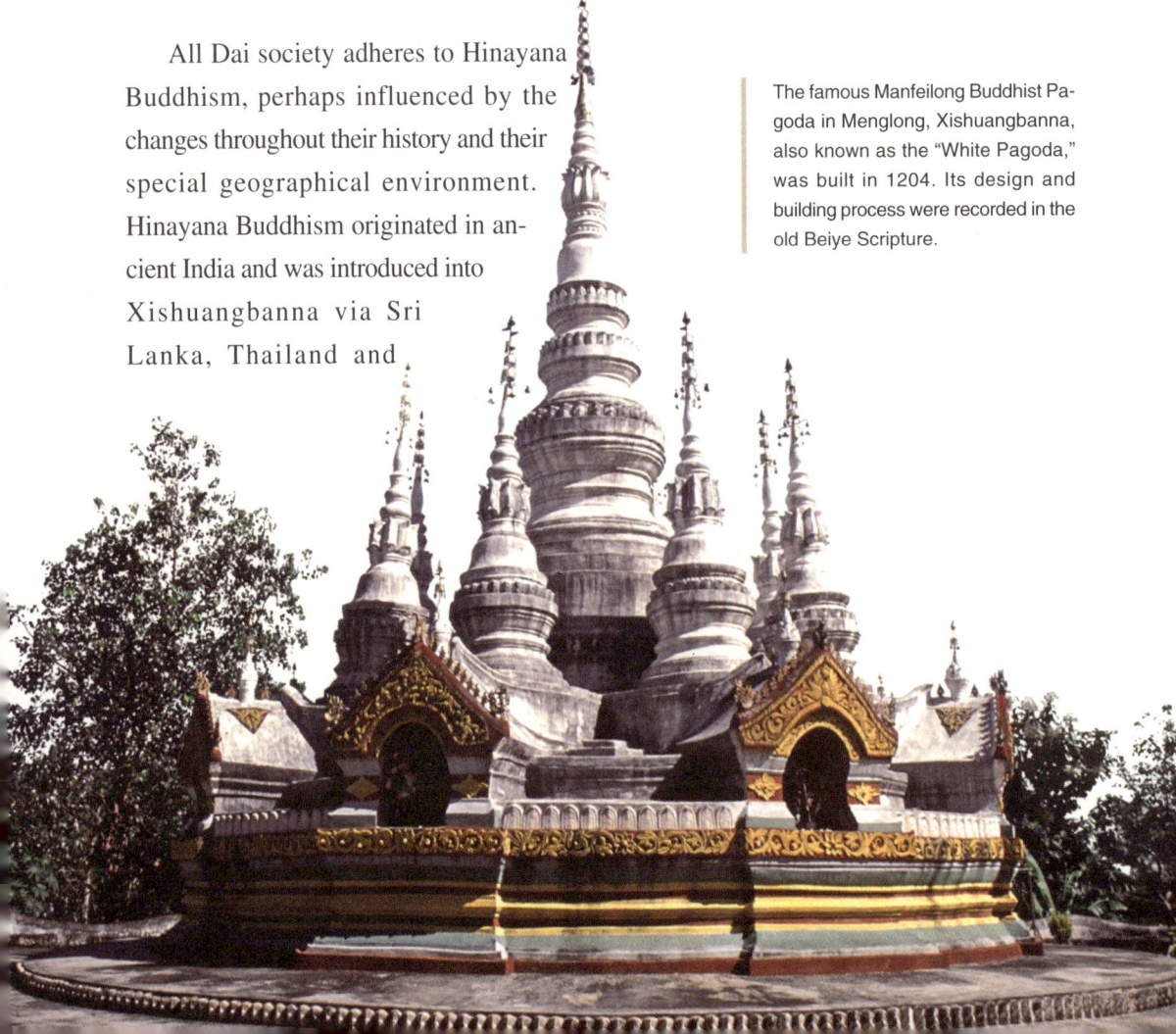

The famous Manfeilong Buddhist Pagoda in Menglong, Xishuangbanna, also known as the "White Pagoda," was built in 1204. Its design and building process were recorded in the old Beiye Scripture.

Myanmar in the third century AD. Its history goes back well over a thousand years.

When Hinayana Buddhism was just introduced into the Dai area, the Dai people resisted it at first because they already had a local, primitive religion. But once Hinayana Buddhism won the support of those with power, a large number of temples were established and the faith gradually came to dominate the political, economic and cultural life of the Dai people.

Historically, Dai culture is concentrated in Buddhist temples. Over 84,000 volumes of ancient pattra-leaf sutras are kept in Xishuangbanna's temples. Many monks are expert in Dai-language scriptures, astronomy and calendars, medicines and healthcare, and are respected as the most learned persons. When local people have problems they will usually consult a monk. Buddha is revered by Dai people everywhere.

Buddhist monasteries also appeal to the Dai because of their easy-going religious discipline: monks are allowed simply to shave their heads without being branded with burning incense as a sign of leaving behind the world and they can marry if they resume secular life. To the traditional Dai way of thinking, unless a man lives a secluded religious life away from family for some part of his life and becomes a cultivated person, he is not qualified to get married. This custom is very different from Buddhist belief in other regions.

According to Dai religious tradition, at the age of seven or eight boys shave their heads and become monks and be-

gin to live a religious life. Girls are not obliged to become nuns, but they are still very pious. Sending off children to monasteries to become monks is a big thing, involving a grand ritual. Once the child becomes a monk, he lives and eats in the monastery, reading scriptures and studying various subjects every day. He does not have to do manual labor outside the monastery but lives on donations from local people. After finishing his daily assignment, he can go out to visit friends and relatives, but may not spend the night outside the monastery. If he wishes, he can stay in the monastery for one, two, even 10 or more years.

It is "illegal" for Dai people to hold a wedding, funeral, or build a house without a monk there to chant Buddhist scriptures. The elderly make daily visits to the temple to present flowers and worship Buddha, to burn incense and pray, hoping to form a better bond with Heaven in their next life.

The Dai people themselves live very simply but are generous in what they give to the temples and monasteries as devotional offerings from followers of Buddha. Twice daily, when the bell rings, households take turns to send their best dishes to the temples. The food of the whole monastery is provided by the entire hamlet.

It is no exaggeration to say that every Dai hamlet has a Buddhist temple; Encircled by shady green forest, every hamlet has a majestic and resplendent palace at its center occupying the best and most spacious spot, presenting a scene unique to Dai hamlets. The architectural style of these temples is similar to the Bamboo stilt houses, bright and colorful, tier upon tier, they seem about to fly.

A Buddhist temple usually consists of three parts: first is the great hall, where worshippers can chant scriptures and pray to Buddha. On the throne in the middle sits a gilded Buddha statue called "Pa Zhao," namely Buddha. On the walls are vivid mu-

Offering to Buddha Festival

rals with true to life depictions of Buddhist tales; second is the place where monks live and study; the third is a depository of Buddhist scriptures, where many Buddhist classics and other books are kept.

Inside every temple you are sure to find Dai brocade hangings, over three meters in length, embroidered with simple images of hunters, princes, elephants and peacocks in elegant colors, embodying the devotion of the Buddhist faithful. Every temple has between 10 and 20 or so resident monks who preach the faith, burn incense and welcome those coming to pray.

Dai temples are full of life and vitality. The larking around of the little monks, the chanting of the scriptures, fill the adjoining hamlet with vitality too. Older monks have wider contact with the world; sporting sunglasses, they ride their bicycles with a girl on the back to catch a movie downtown, or up to the mountains to drive away muntjac deer. They have the same freedom as non-monks.

For Buddhists, temples and pagodas are a spiritual mainstay, and some Dai people even have pagoda tattoos. In Xishuangbanna, pagodas are a type of religious architecture, and are everywhere. The most majestic and splendid of these is the Manfeilong Multi-Pagoda.

The Dai's most lively religious festivals are the "Offering to Buddha Festival" where people donate money or objects to temples praying to Buddha to eliminate disaster and send fortune. There are no fixed times, no fixed places; any place can hold offertory ceremonies and neighboring hamlets are welcome to join in. Presenting quantities of flowers, wines and food to Buddha, people worship, listen devoutly to the scriptures and pray. With night come the firecrackers, Kongming flying lanterns, peacock and golden-deer dances — a veritable paradise for little monks.

◂ Manchunmán Buddhist Temple in Jinghong

▸ Dai people flying Kongming lamps

The Most Recently Confirmed Ethnic Group

In 1979, the Jino ethnic group formally was confirmed by the State Council as China's 56th ethnic minority. Since then there have been no further groups recognized. With a small population of 18,000, the Jino live on Jinuo Mountain in Jinghong City, in Xishuangbanna Autonomous Prefecture, When the People's Republic of China was established in 1949, the Jino ethnic minority was still living in rural communities at a transitional stage between late primitive and class societies. After the founding of New China, it progressed directly into a socialist society. These days, it has its own home-grown leaders, university students, doctors and businessmen, as well as agricultural and sci-tech personnel.

The word Jino means "descendents of uncles" or "race that respects uncles" and the language belongs to the Tibetan-Burmese group of the Sino-Tibetan languages. There is no written language. Jino history and culture are transmitted orally from generation to generation, through stories, folk songs and traditional customs.

The Jino people believe in primitive religion, worship Nature and ancestors, believing that all living creatures have souls and that there are spirits everywhere — spirits of land, mountain and valley. The Jino people have many taboos

▲ Jino woman weaving
◄ Jino man

about land, animals and plants — a "virtual conservation policy" for the local ecological environment and living creatures.

The Jino hold the elderly in great respect: every hamlet has a patriarch and matriarch to manage community affairs. They worship the sun. Their most important ritual instrument is the sun drum with an array of 17 wooden tubes symbolizing rays of light. They think of the sun drum as a reincarnation of god and a symbol of the hamlet, believing that it can bless the entire hamlet. Usually the sun drum is enshrined in the home of the patriarch or matriarch; no one can touch it without permission. Only at the Spring Festival and other special occasions, can the sun drum be taken out for the sun drum dance, the most representative dance of the Jino people.

YUNNAN

Jino people of both sexes like to wear big earrings and they have big ear-piercing holes. They think the size of the ear perforations is symbolic of diligence so they have their ears pierced when they are young and the holes get bigger as their age increases. They also like wearing fabric with blue, red and black patterns woven by themselves.

The Jino people are honest and hospitable and keep to their generous ways: if a hunter catches something, he will share the raw meat with people he meets on the way home and share the cooked meat until it's all eaten. The same goes for drinking alcohol; as long as the guests don't put aside their cups, the host has to drink with them till the end.

The Jino get their livelihood from farming, their traditional crops being rice, cotton and corn. They also have a long history of tea growing, producing the renowned Pu'er tea.

◂▴ Jino ethnic minority's Temaoke Festival

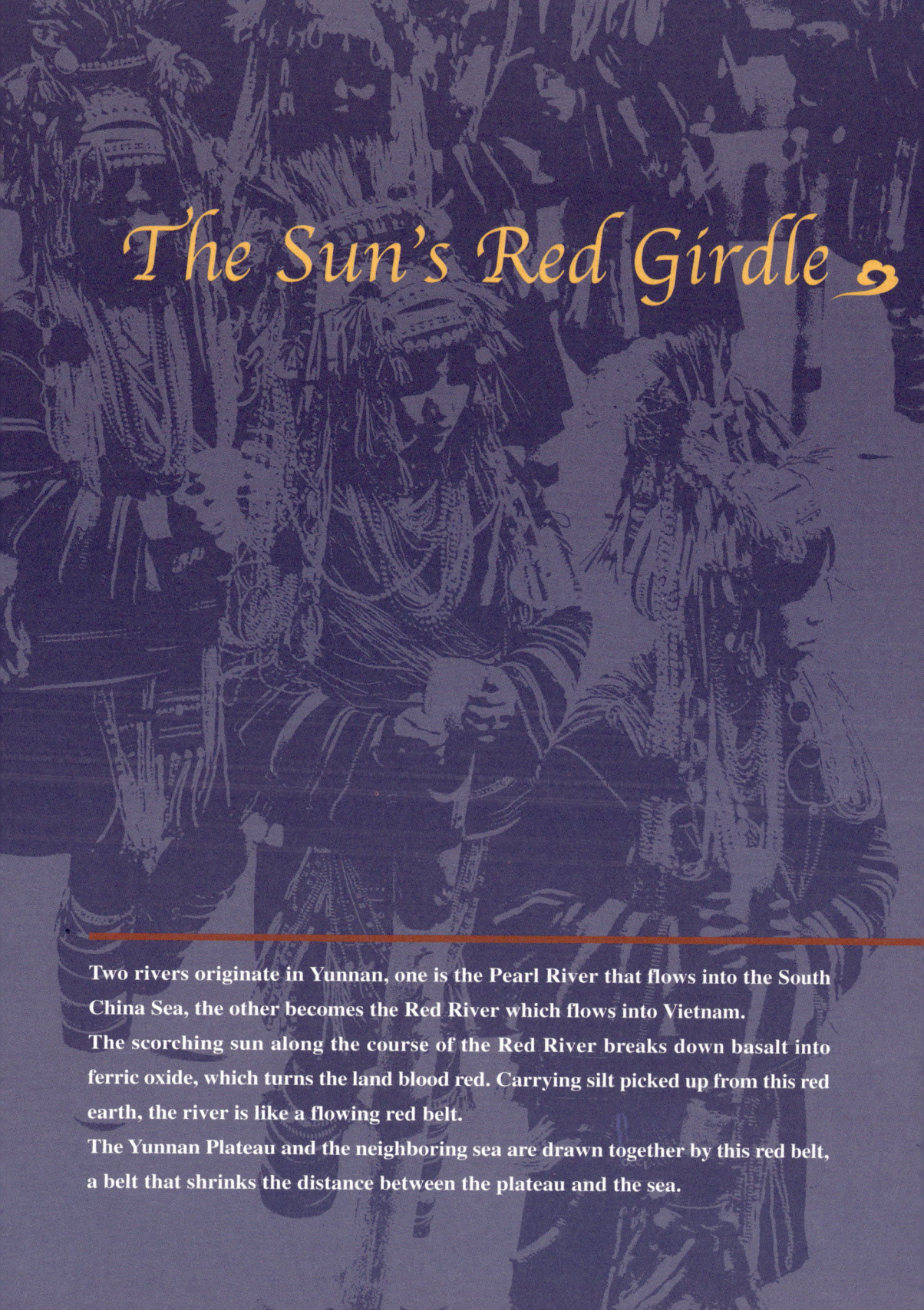

The Sun's Red Girdle

Two rivers originate in Yunnan, one is the Pearl River that flows into the South China Sea, the other becomes the Red River which flows into Vietnam.

The scorching sun along the course of the Red River breaks down basalt into ferric oxide, which turns the land blood red. Carrying silt picked up from this red earth, the river is like a flowing red belt.

The Yunnan Plateau and the neighboring sea are drawn together by this red belt, a belt that shrinks the distance between the plateau and the sea.

Moon Dance by Axi (branch of the Yi ethnic minority) people

Walking Along the Red River

The Red River's upper reaches are called the Lishe River; a little downstream it becomes the Yuanjiang River; as it enters southern Yunnan, it becomes more markedly red and is called the Red River. It has a total length of 692 km in Yunnan Province and 508 km in Vietnam where it empties into the Beibu Gulf. It is very smooth without shoals or rapids.

The Red River

Manhao is an important entrepot center close to the Yunnan-Vietnam border. The French explorer Henri d'Orl'ans came to Vietnam in the 19th century and came to Manhao traveling upstream along the Red River. He left the following record:

Long trade caravans passed by, one after another. Their cattle were yoked with chains hung with bells and decorated by two red tassels. The lead animal bore special ornaments — a small mirror and a crescent-shaped horn. Coming from Mengzi, the cattle train had to walk for over 10 days, each beast carrying over 100 kg of goods and two plates of tin.

Heavily laden mules came and went too. By my reckoning 130 mules passed by a single morning, carrying tin to Manhao and bringing cloth, yarn and tobacco leaves back.

I was amazed by the commercial activities here. We know that in 1894 the tonnage was 5,886 tons. Now I calculated there were 53 ships along the banks. I asked a telegrapher who could speak reasonable English for some information. He said that, in Manhao Township there were about 200 houses, seven tin business bosses who each purchased two or three hundred "piles" of tin plates a year; each "pile" had 50 plates, and each plate weighed 36 kg. In Gejiu mine area, a load (60 kg) of tin was sold at 20 liang (1 liang= 37.5 grams) silver. The transportation charge for a mule from Mengzi to Manhao was six qian (1 qian= 3.75

grams) to one liang of silver. There were also bosses specializing in Vietnamese Lao Cai—Hanoi transportation. After taking tin to Hong Kong, the merchants of Manhao would bring back 10 to 20 thousand packages of goods every year, including cotton threads, cloth, flannels and Guangdong tobacco.

When I was in Manhao, there happened to be the local market held once every six days. Villagers converged on the market from all around. It was very busy. We saw so many different villagers. On the stone stairs on the right bank of the Red River are the most new, strange things. A woman was wearing a Han-style robe embroidered with red and green patterns; her head was bound around with a headdress covered in pieces of silver the size of

Border trading in Hekou County

YUNNAN

a nail and ornamented on each side with three shells and red tassels. The Tibetan nomads had the same ornaments and colors. Some Yao women were even stranger. They wore a round straw hats on top of their hair buns, similar to the straw hats worn by Vietnamese soldiers. The hats were hung with white tassels... People pointed out some Hani women wearing long, knee-length robes; on their chests hung a round silvery disc on which was a motif similar to a Scorpio or Cancer zodiac sign.

Farmers market in Yuanyang County, Honghe Hani and Yi Autonomous Prefecture

Hekou Port. Cross-border trading is an important part of Yunnan's external trade. These days, cross-border trade takes the form of small-scale border trading, border area economic and technological cooperation, and reciprocal local markets. Yunnan cross-border trade with Burma, Laos and Vietnam is brisk.

YUNNAN

Over a century later, nothing has changed but the environment. High standard roads have been opened between Mengzi and Gejiu and Manhao. A reinforced concrete bridge now spans the Red River and many new buildings have risen on both banks. Manhao has become a wholesale center for tropical fruit, with mountains of bananas, grapefruit and walnuts carried away by trucks rather than caravans. Tin produced in Gejiu, "the tin city of China," more than 30 km away, is taken by train to all parts of the world.

The Red River winds up its way to Hekou on the China-Vietnam border, the biggest port in Yunnan.

Across the river from Hekou is Lao Cai in Vietnam. A large road-rail bridge connects the two countries and peoples.

Like its climate, Hekou's cross-border trade is hot all year round. Merchants from over 30 Chinese provinces and cities who have bases here, and foreign merchants stationed at Hekou, fill trucks and ships with their goods. Foreign imports of rubber shoes, battle fatigues, helmets, telescopes, even military knives and camping hammocks (originally produced in different regions for military use) are now all sold to civilians. The small Yunnan-Vietnam Railway built by the French in the 19th century still runs every day from Kunming to Hekou before crossing the Red River Bridge and going on to Hanoi. "The train running slower than the car" is one of the "18 strange things in Yunnan."

The Yunnan-Vietnam Railroad

Railroad bridge between Hekou County and Lao Cai in Vietnam

The Yunnan-Vietnam Railroad starts from Hanoi in Vietnam, goes over the Red River to Hekou, the border city on the Chinese side, before heading directly north to Kunming. Of its overall length of 800 km, the Yunnan section between Hekou and Kunming is 465 km.

At the end of the 19th century, when the citi-

YUNNAN

zens of Paris still thought of subway trains as underground monsters, France won the privilege of constructing and operating railroads in Yunnan from the Qing government. It was an epoch-making revolution for ancient, mysterious Yunnan to accept this European culture and new technology that was so completely different from Chinese tradition. In the process, Chinese and Westerners alike were to pay an unimaginable cost.

Hekou, the last city on the border of southern Yunnan, faces Lao Cai in Vietnam on

| Bisezhai Station on the Yunnan-Vietnam railroad

the opposite bank. The 465-km-long Chinese section of the railroad starts its way north from here, the six-year construction project starting officially in January 1904.

In the context of French technology and manufacturing over a century ago, the construction of a several-hundred-km long railroad through the red-earth mountain plateau of Yunnan called for political will allied with vision, courage and hard work; without these, one of the most magnificent projects in the history of railroad construc-

tion would not have been possible.

This railroad represents the highest level of engineering technology in the early 20th century. For 80 percent of its length it runs between perilous and precipitous mountains. Within a linear distance of 200-km, between Hekou at 76 m above sea level to Mengzi at 2000 m above sea level, there is an altitude disparity of over 1,900 m; the section between Baogu to Baizhai involves a climb of 1,200 m within just 44 km. It has never been equaled in

▲ Hani mother and her daughter on a small train
▶ Hani minority Bamboo Tube Dance

YUNNAN

the history of world railway engineering.

In order to complete the project at the least time and cost, the Hekou to Kunming project was divided into 12 separate sections which were progressed simultaneously.

The French Yunnan-Vietnam Railway Construction Company recruited more than 60,000 Chinese laborers from all over China and there were over 3,000 French, American, British, Italian and Canadian engineers involved in the construction. Along this 465-km-long railway, 107 permanent railway bridges of various types were built and 155 tunnels excavated; 1.66 million cubic m of earth and stones were dug out and over 3,000 temporary bridges and haulage routes built.

For over six years, the fates of over 60,000 Chinese workers and 3,000 foreign technicians were bound up with the railroad. The difficulties they encountered were beyond the imagination of the decision-makers in Paris.

The climate was sweltering, particularly around the Nanxi River valley

area, where summer temperatures could exceed 40; it was humid and oppressive, and infections from tropical diseases and plague were always possible. Statistics show that during those six years, 12,000 souls lie buried along this 465-km-long track, among which 10,000 died in the Nanxi River valley, most of them Chinese laborers who gave up their lives in order to earn a living. There were also several hundred Frenchmen and other foreigners, drawn from afar by this railroad, who never made it back to their native soil.

One of many bridges along the route is the 67.15-m-long steel structure railway bridge over the Sicha River in the Nanxi valley. To Chinese, this handsome and delicate structure is known as "Wishbone Bridge." While this structure and the Eiffel Tower in Paris are both products of the technology of that age, when compared with the Eiffel Tower in the famous metropolis of Paris, the "Wishbone Bridge" spanning between two sheer and precipitous peaks seems to be performing a death-defying tightrope dance.

Since its completion in 1909, the "Wishbone Bridge" has never had an adverse impact on railroad traffic. Hardly a bolt has had to be changed.

Hurtling out of the forests with its long "wooh wooh," the steam engine drew remote Yunnan closer to the world at one fell swoop. And from this point on, tranquil Kunming became a city on the international traffic arteries; advanced French steam

YUNNAN

trains would shuttle day and night between Hekou and Kunming, carrying Michelin rubber tires and passenger carriages.

The trains brought various Western goods to the people of southern Yunnan, and filled the commodity markets of Kunming. Well-off families adopted pocket watches and irons; women took to wearing nylon stockings and French bread appeared on the dinner tables; later, in towns along the railroad, black, bitter-tasting coffee became the drink of choice for the elderly when they were chatting.

Between 1911 and 1912, it was via this railroad that Yunnan sent its first groups of students to study in Europe and America. In 1912 Yunnan built its first hydroelectric power station at Shilong (Stone Dragon) Dam, the German generators being imported via this railroad.

In 1918, Kunming introduced technology and equipment from France to build waterworks, making it the first city in China to have tap water. In 1923, telegraph and telephone networks were established in Kunming and international weight units replaced the traditional Chinese measure, the *jin*.

At the same time, the Yunnan-Vietnam Railroad also brought French-style architecture, culture, religion and arts to cities along its route.

Hani Terraces

To go up along the Ailao Range, is like seeing a scroll of different folk customs unroll: in the hot river valley area live the Dai people who transformed that scorching land along the river into a granary; the Yao ethnic minority live in the mountain valleys where the climate is mild, among thriving forests, crystal-clear streams, where fruits and fungi abound. Their medical skills, passed down from generation to generation, are amazing. The Miao mostly live on the mountains. The Miao women have dexterous hands, producing extraordinarily beautiful wax printing and embroidery. The Hani and Yi ethnic groups are concentrated on the cool hillside areas.

The Hani, meaning the "people living in a mountain" are an ancient ethnic group with a long history and rich culture, its people distributed across China, Vietnam, Laos and Myanmar. The Hani population in China numbers 1.25 million half of whom are concentrated in the Ailao Mountain area south of the Red River.

The terraced field agriculture of the Hani ethnic group is an agricultural miracle of the subtropical mountain areas in Yunnan. The splendor of the Hani terraces is the result of toil and moil by generation after generation of diligent Hani farmers. In trying to eke out a living amid the mountain, they created a marvelous feat.

The Hani people settled down to farming a long time ago and they have a very long history of grain cultivation. The epic of the Hani ethnic group describes their ancient homeland thus: "On the high mountains, sow a good three liters of seed. The locusts of high summer can't reach the high mountains, severe frosts and snows of winter won't reach down the plain. The highland fields bring forth harvests to gather, grains grown within our plain are fat and swollen." Back in the Qing Dynasty, the terraced fields created by the Hani people already presented a splendid sight.

Hani hamlets are sited at the temperate mid level of the mountain; the entire lower part of the mountain, from the edge of the hamlet to the river valley at the mountain foot, consists of Hani terraces in various shapes and sizes.

A saying about the Ailao Mountains goes "however high the mountain, the water is the same height." Hani people value the protection of high mountains and forests and in the Ailao Mountains water circulates through the agricultural production system in a special way. On the terraced mountainsides the Hani dig irrigation ditches. Usually, the irrigation ditches can contain the water brought by streams flowing down from the high mountain forest; in the rainy season, water can be held by the irrigation ditches and flow via them into the terraced paddies. Thus, all the levels of paddy terraces can be irrigated and the water finally joins the river in the valley. The sources for the larger irrigation canals are linked to the pools and streams of the high mountain forests. Some are several km long, running through neighboring counties.

Irrigation ditches crisscross the Ailao Mountains on the southern bank of the Red River like a spider's web. To every Ailao Mountains villager they are lifelines, so they are assiduous in maintaining them and anyone spotting a damaged irrigation ditch would fix it.

Now, let's go upstream along the Red River from Manhao, and enter the terraced world of Yuanyang County in the Ailao Mountains.

The terraces here are a wonder. Particularly so in winter and spring, when plot after plot of flooded terrace awaiting planting, radiate gold and silvery light like so many mirrors, level by level, step by step, climbing from the mountain foot so far below you can't see it, repeating and repeating up into the clouds, while water drops down tier by tier, creating thousands of waterfalls, large and small, cascading over every slope.

In winter, when there is a full moon, you'll see not only the miraculous terraced fields, but thousands of round moons reflected on the watery fields. The mushroom-house villages by the terraced fields are quiet, seemingly asleep. Several Hani girls slip out of the hamlet to catch eels in the terraces, trouser legs rolled high and bamboo baskets aslant across their backs. They play boisterous water games, breaking the moon reflections, causing the eels to take flight, the dogs to bark, but attracting their lovers.

▶ The famous Long Street Banquet in the Ailao Mountain area. Every year, after the Spring Festival, the Yi people hold their grand Jiluo Festival, each family preparing a table of delicious dishes and setting it out on the village street. Villagers and guests join together to wish for clement weather and abundant harvests in the coming year. In Habo, a Hani village, 300 households set out 300 closely-touching tables of delicacies of every kind. When guests arrive they are warmly welcomed, eating and drinking with every family.

▶ Terraces, Yuanyang

Galloping Red Bulls

In terms of geography, the Honghe (Red River) is a river; in administrative terms it is the Hani and Yi Autonomous Prefecture; in commercial terms it is also part of many company names.

Red River ads can be seen everywhere in China: a herd of big, powerful red bulls charging hell for leather across a red landscape, in a demonstration of immense collective strength.

"The galloping herd of bulls represents the energy and vigor of Red River employees," said a company spokesperson.

"Red" cigarettes, "Red" wines and "Red" (brown) sugar produced by Red River dominate the mar-

YUNNAN

"Yunnan Red" vineyard
Honghe Cigarette Factory

ket of Honghe Autonomous Prefecture but they are concentrated in Mi Le County.

Mi Le County, whose name means Maitreya, the laughing Buddha, is 120 km or so from Kunming. The Yi people say that "Mi Le" is the transliteration of "red land" in Yi dialect. The Han Chinese say that Maitreya once visited and rested here.

The building of a majestic golden statue of Maitreya on the Jinping Mountain on the outskirts of Mi Le and mainly invested by the Red River Cigarette Company was approved by both Yi and Han people.

Mi Le County, the first county as you enter southern Yunnan, has both ancient streets and modern construction. Asphalt roads extend from here to the important cities of Kaiyuan, Mengzi, Gejiu and the China-Vietnam border cities of Hekou and Wenshan in southern Yunnan.

Cigarettes are a pillar industry of Yunnan and Yunnan Honghe Cigarette Factory is one of the pillars of Yunnan.

Vast acres of sugar cane

"Red wines" produced in Mi Le County consist of "Yunnan Red Wine" and "Yunnan Dry Wine." It was originally a slack state-owned farm, but now it has developed into a 10,000-mu (1 mu = 0.0667 ha) vineyard which is not only a base for grape production but also a scenic spot. At the Grape Festival in August, grapes fill the land and streets — even the flowing water smell of grapes. The Mi Le grape variety came from the old Cigu Church in "Shangri-La" when missionaries brought grapevines and wine-making skills from France and the local people's viniculture and wine-making customs have been handed down to the present day. The makers of Mi Le Yunnan red wine specially send employees to study technology; traditional French winemaking skills combined with modern scientific methods make for the excellent quality and wide popularity of "Yunnan Red" and "Yunnan Dry."

Thanking to the vast "forests" of sugarcane farmland in Mi Le, the county enjoys the reputation of "home of sugar cane," "home of sugar," and supply of "Red" sugar products cannot keep up with demand.

World in a Gourd

The Awa Mountains are like a virgin who has spent long, long years in seclusion. Even now, the sanctity of her "parlor" has remained virtually complete and hidden away from prying eyes, and the dignity of this mysterious realm seems not one to be slighted. For age after age she has confined herself here like the gourd in Wa mythology. Now the barriers have been breached, air and land routes opened up, the mysterious isolated realm has opened up its gates; the new-discovered world within must be most valuable — at once ancient and brand new.

Awa Mountains

YUNNAN

To outsiders the name of the place where the Wa ethnic group is concentrated is known as the Awa Mountains. There are two administrative divisions, the Ximeng Wa Autonomous County and the Cangyuan Wa Autonomous County.

In Wa mythology, a cow gave birth to a gourd, and Man grew from out of the gourd. In the Wa language, this process is called "Sigang Li," "sigang" referring to the gourd and "Li" meaning to emerge; together it means that Man came out from the gourd. Thus, the gourd itself is a very important sacred object for the Wa people.

Since time immemorial, the Awa Mountains have always been an enigma.

According to written records, the Wa mostly "lived in the mountains," "had stockaded villages," "did not use oxen to plough, just women working with hoes," "apart from growing coarse food cereals, hunted their food." Moreover, they "were always moving from one place to the next without any routine." Wa men, "brave, dauntless and agile," used to be a major component of ancient Nanzhao armies, and they "were so brave as a vanguard."

When you really get into the Awa Mountains, you will find that these historical records were too simple. The bald word "mountains" as in "lived in the mountains" stands for scenery and resources that words on a page cannot adequately describe.

The Awa Mountains, with its ridges and peaks rising one after another, look far from barbarous and wild, and are always green whatever the season. Cangyuan County alone has over 33,333 ha of forest. The boundless and continuous tropical rain forests are home to such rare tree species as Toona ciliata, nanmu, camphor tree, Anthocephalus chinensis, Schima superba Gardner & Champ, ferreous mesua, and golden birch.... The Spinulose tree fern, whose leaves look like fern but also resemble rooster tails, is called a "living ancient plant fossil." Birds include the green peafowl, hornbill, Psittacula alexandri, golden pheasant, and

sunbird... Amid these forests elephant, wild boar, and leopard also roam. Without these wild beasts, the tropical rain forest would lose a kind of heroic and powerful vitality. And it is said that the big "Wildman" has been spotted in these mountains.

The Awa mists are constantly changing, varying with the four seasons. In autumn and spring particularly, the mist rises after midnight, floating lightly and gracefully above the mountains, like wispy white gauze covering a stage. Comes the next morning and it is a sea of mist, rivers of dazzling snow and soft fluffy cotton snaking between the valleys, changing into a myriad of forms between the mountains, those lofty mountains becoming islands in a sea of mist. The summer mists are random and undefined, just like milk spilled between the heaven and the earth, covering fields, villages, and woods — engulfing towering mountains too.

▲ Wa minority women

▶ Guangyunmian Temple in Cangyuan

◀ Wa village

The Mystery of the Cangyuan Cliff Paintings

The Cangyuan Cliff Paintings, located in Mengdong River valley in Lincang Wa Autonomous County, cover an area of over 400 sq m, and are among the oldest cliff paintings discovered in China to date.

The cliff paintings are scattered on 11 old cliffs, the earliest discovered in 1965. Despite weathering the elements for over 3,000 years, the colors are still brilliant, a true treasure of primeval art.

The paintings are red in appearance. According to research, they were produced by ancient man using best-quality pigment mixing red iron ore and ox blood which cannot be replicated today.In most of the drawings the color was possibly finger-applied, while the larger ones were possibly painted with feathers or other tools. The color is stable and has not changed over a long period. The drawings are simple and unsophisticated, presenting a bold and spontaneous picture of life in remote antiquity. The paintings mostly depict hunting, dancing, wars, buildings, and villages. In terms of shape, the painters emphasized the basic features of humans and animals. For example, it is easy to identify animal species from features such as horns, ears and tails. Human images are usually expressed with a round head without facial features, and bodies with a simple triangle, except in some cases where body curves are emphasized. But by changing the position of arms and legs, the limbs are painted in

Cangyuan cliff paintings

attitudes of movement; the men and women in the paintings can clearly be made out standing, walking, hunting or dancing.

The cliff paintings reproduce a picture of the life and livelihood of a primitive tribe; they also reflect certain religious concepts. We can see, too, that these cliff paintings had a clear recording function and significance.

The simple Wa people regard these painted cliffs as "holy cliffs" and the paintings themselves as the manifestation of "Buzhuo" — local spirits. Because of the awe in which they hold the spirits, they usually do not approach these cliff paintings. When important festivals come around, they will go to offer sacrifice.

The Warm and Spontaneous Wa

These simple Wa people who consider the cliff paintings as manifestation of the spirits number 347,000 in Yunnan (out of a total Wa population of 351,000). Thus the Wa ethnic group is a particularity of Yunnan.

Like the Awa Mountains the character of the Wa people is bold and unreserved, strong and daring; they treat people with great sincerity. To be a guest in a Wa family is great good luck

YUNNAN

PANORAMIC CHINA

▲ Wa women pounding rice
◂◂ Wa ethnic minority Wood Drum Dance
◂ Wa girl

YUNNAN

since the Wa believe "without wine, no courtesy" and that "without hot spice, no good dish." So the host's hospitality can only be proved by the guest getting totally sozzled, his head dripping with sweat from the spicy food. In the Awa Mountains there are as many pipes as there are people; these stretch into a big wine jar like drinking straws for people to drink the "soaking wine." There is tea at the side for those with limited capacity for alcohol. There is a special Awa Mountains way of drinking tea too: take some tea leaves, throw them into a pottery teapot and heat this over a fire pit until the leaves give off their fragrance; only then pour a bowl of water into the pot, which immediately emits a great "schhhhhhhh" and the heady aroma of the tealeaves fills the room. The host offers it ceremoniously to the guest, having drunk from it first, so as to prove that the tea is neither poisonous nor harmful. This shows the Wa people's honesty and simplicity.

The Wa have no written language, and express emotions through material objects; gifts of banana, sugarcane, brown sugar, salt, tea and tobacco symbolize intimacy and friendship; hot peppers show anger and breakup; chicken feathers mean urgency; gunpowder and live charcoal are a declaration of war...In the past the heroic and valiant Wa people used to protect their territory together with warriors of other ethnic groups.

The Wa like to sing and dance. Common dances include the Circle, Long Hair, and Rice-Husking dances. On New Year's Day or at other festivals, they will spontaneously gather together for three

days of singing and dancing. The Wa girls' uninhibited and energetic Long Hair Dance and Foot Stamping Dance are classic symbols of the Awa Mountains.

As with most minority groups in Yunnan, the Wa believe that all things — mountains, rivers and trees — have their deities and that living creatures have their souls. The biggest religious event of the year is "pulling the wooden drum." The wooden drum is a holy object worshipped by the Wa, which they consider as "an instrument to reach the gods." They firmly believe that beating the drum has magical powers to summon them. "Pulling the wooden drum" originates from the practical need of getting a new drum to replace the old one when it is broken. Under the leadership of the village head, the entire village sings and dances until midnight, then goes up the mountain to fell and bring back a tree of the right quality and auspicious *fengshui,* then fashion a drum from the tree while they pray. The drum is made by opening a deep split at the top of the trunk, then digging down and hollowing it out to a special shape. In this way the trunk becomes a holy object, the Wa believing that it will bring seasonable weather and good harvests to the Awa Mountains.

The Wa are good at carving; carved images of human or animals can be seen everywhere in their villages. They love red and black, always wearing black garments and red ornaments. Both sexes wear tattoos: Wa men usually have bird, flower, cattle or tiger tattoos below the neck or on the chest, back, arms and legs, while the women have flowers and plant tattoos below the neck or on their limbs.

| Wa weavers

Fragrant Land

Yunnan has an old international pack-horse road that leads to Tibet, India, and Pakistan... and the main commodity traded on this ancient route was tea.

Yunnan, with its year-round seas of mist and mountains of cloud, its fertile earth and fresh mountain streams, is a paradise for growing tea.

Yunnan is one of the world's major tea gardens; the Lancang River valley including Fengqing, Lincang and Shuangjiang, is one of the places

YUNNAN

▲ Wa people picking tea
◄ Aini people picking tea

where the tea plant originated. A 2,500 year-old colony of ancient wild tea plants, covering more than 320 ha, has been discovered at Mengku in Shuangjiang. The Benshan tea tree of Xinyuan and the big tea tree discovered at Xiangzhuqing Mountain in Fengqing are more than 3,750 years old. Furthermore, the thousand-year-old big tea tree at Bangwei Village of Fudong Township in Lancang County, is a transitional type between wild and cultivated species, and still produces leaves today. In April 1993, 181 tea experts from nine countries

Fengqing — the source of "Dianhong" tea

examined this ancient tea tree and reached the world-shaking conclusion that tea originated, not in India, but in Yunnan, China.

Historically the tea-producing areas of Yunnan were concentrated at Pu'er in southern Yunnan and at Fengqing in western Yunnan, Pu'er producing mainly green tea, Fengqing mainly black.

The capital of the area in which Pu'er is located is "the tea capital" Simao. In fact, Pu'er itself does not produce much tea and the major production area is Xishuangbanna, particularly Menghai. Because of Xishuangbanna's remoteness and the Lancang River was a barrier to road traffic, the caravans would take the leaves to be processed at Pu'er 180

YUNNAN

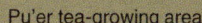
Pu'er tea-growing area

km away, from where it would be transported to other places as finished product. This is how the name of Pu'er Tea won its world fame.

Fengqing, which produces black tea, was called Shunning in ancient times. The earliest record of its tea growing is in the *Book of Barbarians* written by Fan Zhuo in the Tang Dynasty, the term "barbarians" referring to ethnic minorities in Yunnan. The book describes tea growing in the Lancang River valley.

The "Yunnan Black Tea" produced in Fengqing sells in Asia, Europe, Oceania and the Americas. In 1986 when Britain's Queen Elizabeth II visited Yunnan, the provincial governor presented her with a gift of "Superfine Kong Fu Yunnan Black Tea."

▲ Tea plantation
▲ Qizi cake tea
◀ Pu'er tea

Home of Eternal Spring

Sunshine as lazy as a cat, random rain that falls at will, create the dry and rainy seasons in a year without distinction between spring and autumn, winter and summer. In this mild and clement climate the people of Kunming lead their lives at a leisurely pace. Both unhurried history and comfortable modern life continue on ad infinitum. The most vital and energetic element are the fresh flowers; throughout the year, whatever the season, they cover the city balconies and clothe the fields beyond; sometimes, you can't decline them, even if you want to.

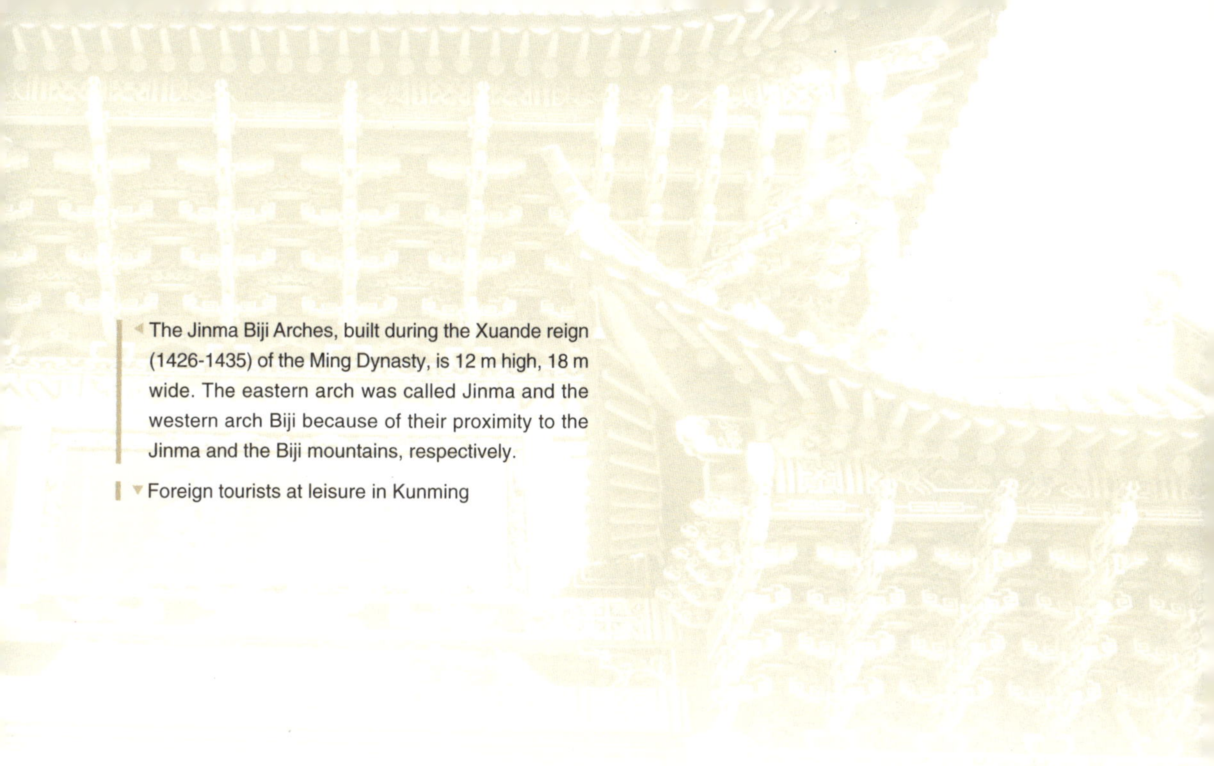

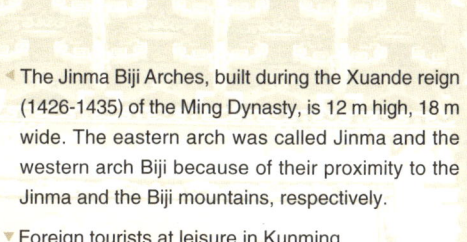

◀ The Jinma Biji Arches, built during the Xuande reign (1426-1435) of the Ming Dynasty, is 12 m high, 18 m wide. The eastern arch was called Jinma and the western arch Biji because of their proximity to the Jinma and the Biji mountains, respectively.

▼ Foreign tourists at leisure in Kunming

Kunming

Kunming, the capital city of Yunnan, is surrounded by mountains on three sides and adjoins Dianchi Lake to the south. It covers an area of 15,000 sq km. For reasons of its year-round mild climate, Kunming is known as the "City of Eternal Spring."

The history of Yunnan can be traced back to the third century BC while that of Kunming goes back over 1,200 years. For century after century since the end of the Dali Kingdom, Kunming has remained the political, cultural and economic center of Yunnan, and the communications hub for trade on Yunnan-Guizhou Plateau. The Italian traveler Marco Polo praised it as "a magnificent metropolis."

With the vigorous growth of commerce, Kunming's former simplicity has given way to bustle, high buildings and vitality. But within the city, places of cultural interest and histori-

YUNNAN

cal relics, scenic spots, and ethnic minority communities lend Kunming a unique charm where the old and new live side by side.

In recent years, Kunming has gone all out to promote international tourism. Particularly in the years since the World Horticultural Exposition which it hosted in May 1999, Kunming has become an international metropolis and a fashionable, alluring city.

Waves of people from other Chinese provinces have come to Kunming to do business, for example: people from Jiangsu and Zhejiang are engaged in clothing and jewelry; Guangdong people run beauty and hair salons; Fujian people deal in building materials; people from Sichuan and Guizhou are mostly laborers. These people work together for the development of Kunming.

Kunming is the economic, business and trade and distribution center of Yunnan. As such it has created many "firsts" in the China's modern industrial history, including "the first hydropower station," "the first telescope," and "the first power cable." Kunming is renowned too for its computer automated precision machine tools, wires and cables, optical instruments, cigarettes, *baiyao* traditional medicine, and *weiqi* chess sets which sell to over 40 countries

◄ Newly-weds on Jinma Biji Plaza

▼ By the end of 1999, Yunnan had 110,000 km of roads open to traffic, the most in China, representing nearly 1/10 of China's total road length.

such as the United States and Japan. Kunming also abounds in rice, wheat, oil plants, tobacco and corn, and thus is renowned as the "Granary of Central Yunnan."

Kunming is the provincial center of science, technology, education and culture. It is home to over 200 research institutes and 16 institutions of higher learning, responsible for training qualified personnel and developing technologies for the economic and social development of Yunnan.

Kunming has twinned with cities such as Fujisawa (Japan), Zurich (Switzerland), Chef Chauveon (Morocco), Denver (USA), Wagga Wagga (Australia), Cochabamba (Bolivia), Chiang Mai (Thailand), and Mandalay (Myanmar).

People lose their hearts to Kunming, a lively city permeated with the fragrance of flowers.

Dounan in Kunming is the largest flower center in China. Roses, camellias, Casablanca lilies, carnations, gypsophilia.... Every day at dawn, the flower market at Dounan is a sea of

Dounan Flower Market. "If you never come to Yunnan, you'll never know how beautiful flowers can be; if you never come to Dounan, you'll never know how cheap they can be," as Chinese flower dealers say. Dounan is Asia's largest flower market.

bobbing heads and booming business. Every day boxes and sheathes of flowers, beautifully packaged, are shipped off to Beijing, Shanghai, Japan, Hong Kong, Macao, Guangzhou.... The supply of Kunming flowers falls short of demand. At festivals and holidays, Kunmingers like to ride out to Dounan to appreciate and buy flowers there. Flowers are calculated by bundle and on Valentine's Day, people send their sweethearts a bundle of romantic roses instead of a single rose. But then, a bundle of roses in Kunming is cheaper than a single rose in Beijing....

Kunming people, in their comfortable climate, favor mountains and rivers. They know how to enjoy their leisure time — drinking tea, climbing mountains, collecting and eating mountain delicacies.... They have none of the fatigue of metropolitan living, so most of them have no desire to leave.

Compared with other Chinese cities, Kunming has a climate of eternal spring and an excellent eco-environment. By dint of continually improving its people's living environment and maintaining its traditional cultural character, Kunming is striving to become one of the "world's best cities to live in."

| The site of South-West Associated University at Yunnan Normal University | Yunnan Normal University today |

The forerunner of today's Yunnan Normal University was the South-West Associated University. During World War II, Kunming became the center of higher learning in China, and it was home for eight years to eminent specialists in education, arts and culture. Famous universities such as Peking, Tsinghua and Nankai universities moved to Kunming and large numbers of students and top minds braved the rigors of the journey to come here and found "the South-West Associated University" which trained many famous scholars and experts for poor and undeveloped China. They achieved great things for the development of China's science and technology and culture. Conditions were tough but teachers and students were not just seeking education; they saw China's survival as their responsibility. Despite its short history the spirit of the South-West Associated University is precious and memorable in any age.

Some teachers and students of the South-West Associated University:

Physicists; Chen-ning Yang and Tsung-dao Lee—winners of the Nobel Prize for Physics; Deng Jiaxian—the theoretical designer of China's first A-bomb who made great contributions to China's atomic and hydrogen bombs; Wang Xiji (Bai ethnic group)—chief designer of China's first recoverable remote sensing satellite; Huang Hongjia—master of optical cable; Tu Shou'e—chief designer of the Long March II carrier rocket; Tang Aoqing—founder of China's quantum chemistry; Huang Kun—founder of China's semiconductor industry; Ci Yungui—pioneer of China's computer industry....

In 1955, of the first batch of 400 academicians put forward by the Chinese Academy of Science over 180 were teachers or alumni of the South-West Associated University.

Today, Yunnan has 80 domestic and international routes and Kunming has the fourth biggest airport in China.

Every November, flocks of seagulls fly from Siberia to Cuihu Lake to over-winter in balmy Kunming, before returning in March. The gulls have been coming to the Spring City for 18 years running.

The West Mountain and Dianchi Lake

The vast Dianchi Lake, also called Kunming Lake, lies southwest of the city. It is Yunnan's biggest plateau lake, measuring approximately 40 km from north to south, 8 km from east to west, and with an average depth of 4 m. It is fed by over 20 rivers and its waters finally flow into the Jinsha River.

A sleeping beauty lies alongside the lake. On clear days, you can see her graceful presence, visible above the fields, above the high buildings, in morning sun or sunset clouds.

She lies to the west of the lake, whose vast waters form her soft and comfortable bed, supporting her plump body. Her long cascading tresses floating upon the water; her straight nose, proud bosom, flat stomach... a real sleeping beauty. Lying in the eternal spring of Kunming, she has weathered the winds and rains of millennium after millennium.

She is a Venus in repose. A famous mountain, too — the West Mountain.

YUNNAN

The West Mountain is also called Biji Mountain. Biji, literally meaning green rooster, is phoenix in local legend.

It is the city's most magnificent and beautiful mountain with lush forests of bamboo, pine and cypress, in whose deep and tranquil depths are hidden the Huating and Taihua temples. Halfway up the mountain is the burial place of the "people's musician" Nie Er who composed the music for China's national anthem. Nie Er was born in Yuxi on the opposite bank of the lake.

The most soul-stirring sight on the West Mountain are the Longmen Grottoes "standing on a platform opened on the sheer cliff." These were started in 1781 by stonemasons who came from the foot of the West Mountain. Working suspended on ropes between these towering cliffs, they spent over 20 years chiseling and hollowing out magnificent and strange fairy rooms, Buddhist pavilions, reliefs and stone statues, all combined in a harmonious whole.

Standing by the Longmen Grottoes, one can see the vast Dianchi Lake stretching out to the foot of distant green mountains. On both banks deep green trees surround the farmers' homes, and it's hard to tell whether this is the human world or paradise. One cannot help but bring to mind of the peerless verses hanging on the Grand View Pavilion on West Mountain:

"The Five hundred li Dianchi Lake unrolls before my eyes. Wearing my headdress high and throwing out my chest, how happy I am to see the water's vast expanse! Look! the

▲ The Grand View Pavilion was built in 1682, eight years after a monk had built a temple to Guanyin here. The governor of Yunnan thought this the best spot to enjoy the views over lakes and mountains, so he had pavilions built here, of which the Grand View Pavilion is the most famous. It contains a long (180-character) paired couplet by the Qing Dynasty writer Sun Ranweng. Although he lived poor, he always cared about people.

◄ Sleeping beauty

Gold Steed galloping in the east, the Green Phoenix flying in the west, the Long Snake serpentine in the north and the White Crane gliding in the south. Brilliant talents may come to this height and enjoy the views, visit the crab- or shell-like isles, so like beauties with hair out-flowing in the air or veiled in mist, where reeds and duckweed spread out towards the sky, dotted with green-feathered birds and rainbow clouds. Why not drink in the fragrant paddy-fields all around, the sparkling fine sand far and near, the slender lotus of late summer and the swaying willows of early spring!

The events of past millennia flood into my mind. A cup of wine in hand and facing immensity, I sigh, for how many heroes have passed away with the rolling waves. Remember the Han warships maneuvering, the iron pillar erected in the Tang, the jade axes that

pacified the frontier in the Song and the armored horsemen's expeditions in the Yuan. Valiant deeds have exhausted mountain-moving strength, but pearl screens and painted beams last no longer than morning clouds and evening rain, stone tablets and monuments lie in shattered ruin, buried in grizzly smoke and the sun's departing rays. What remains is only an occasional bell sounding in the cold hills, the lamplights of fishermen flickering by the riverside, two lines of wild geese flying in autumn sky and a melancholy dream of hoary winter frost."

The trials and hardships of history are now the stuff of casual conversational reminiscence, enhancing the nostalgic atmosphere. This thousand-year sleeping beauty is now history's only witness; she is moved by, but her eyes cannot fully take in, the new spectacle, the sparkling lights from the many high-rise towers that now line the lake-shore.

Statue of the people's musician Nie Er

Meet the Great Zheng He

Five hundred years ago, there were few people in remote Yunnan who know how big the boundless sea was, and while plateau people dared climb thousands of mountains they dared not brave sea voyages. The first person to change this situation was Zheng He from Yunnan, China's first navigator; starting in 1405 he was to make seven voyages to the Western Seas within 28 years.

Zheng He was born in 1371 in Kunyang (today's Jinning County) by the side of Dianchi Lake. At the age of 11, he was captured by troops that the founding emperor of the Ming Dynasty Zhu Yuanzhang had sent to stabilize Yunnan and was taken to the capital where he was made a eunuch. Zheng He, of Muslim Hui ethnicity, had the original family name of Ma, after his father Ma Hazhi; his new surname Zheng was bestowed by the emperor.

The 15th century in China was an age of peace and prosperity. The Ming Emperor Chengzu, Zhu Di, a man of great talent and bold vision, was "determined to open the four seas," and thus created the great mission of Zheng He's history-making voyages.

Zheng He's fleet for his first voyage included 62 larges ships and their crews totaling

YUNNAN

28,000 men. The biggest ship, 44.4 *zhang* (147 m) long and 18 *zhang* (59 m) wide, had nine masts and 12 sails; they had a capacity of 800 tons and could carry 1,000 people. The fleet achieved three world superlatives: the largest ocean-going fleet, the most advanced nautical instruments, and the most advanced warship escorts.

Within those 28 years, Zheng He and his fleets visited more than 30 countries including what are now Japan, Thailand, Cambodia, the Philippines, Indonesia, India, Sri Lanka, as well as the Red Sea and countries along Africa's southeast coast. It was a tremendous achievement that opened a new page in Chinese navigation history.

Ninety-two years later, the Portuguese explorer Vasco da Gama's four sail ships reached the Indian Ocean from the Atlantic by rounding the southern tip of Africa. Eighty-seven years later, Christopher Columbus landed in North America and discovered the New World. Between 1519 and 1522 Ferdinand Magellan circumnavigated the globe discovering that the earth is actually a sphere covered with water and its landmasses are a single but interrupted entity.

This great navigator is worshiped as a god in Sanbao temples, Sanbao caves and at Sanbao wells around the world, and the statue of Zheng He at Zheng He Park in Kunyang shows the respect with which he is remembered by the people of his hometown.

◄ Statue of the navigator Zheng He
◄◄ Tomb of Ma Hazhi, Zheng He's father

Visit Ashma

Three hundred million years ago, the Yunnan-Tibet Plateau was still a sea. Later, due to crustal movement, rocks at the bottom of the sea gradually rose up to form mountains. The erosive effect of wind and rain over several hundred thousand years has carved this limestone into thousands of lava pillars, forming towering peaks. With the biggest concentration of such rocks, the Stone Forest in Lunan County is a

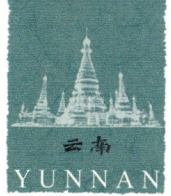
YUNNAN

famous scenic spot.

The Stone Forest, covering an area of some 30,000 ha, was first discovered in the Ming Dynasty and was officially designated as "Stone Forest" during the Kangxi reign period (1662-1722) of the Qing Dynasty. Its complex geomorphology has generated fantastic peaks and rocks in every shape and posture. Enter the Stone Forest and everything can stir your imagination — those fantastic lofty rocks are a great source for myth and poetry.

The Stone Forest's "Ashma Rock" embodies a moving love story. Ashma was a beautiful Yi maiden who loved a courageous young man called Ahay. Unfortunately a landlord's son took a fancy to Ashma and kidnapped her. Ahay came to her rescue, but they were separated once more by mountain torrents. Ultimately the sorrowful and wrathful Ashma was transformed into a rock awaiting her lover.

The Torchlight Festival, the Yi ethnic group's biggest festival, is held every year on the 24th day in the sixth month of the lunar calendar. During the day they have beauty contests, horse racing, and archery; at night they hold torches high aloft, singing and dancing the whole night through. Chinese and foreign tourists are drawn to join in these revelries and enjoy them to the full.

Elsewhere in Yunnan, the Sand Forest of Luliang and the Earth Forest of Yuanmou can rival the Stone Forest.

▲ Ashma Rock in the Stone Forest

◄ The spectacular Stone Forest, in Lunan County, 100 km from Kunming. It is the world's highest single karst formation.

The Yi people are the most populous ethnic minority in Yunnan, mainly living in Chuxiong Yi Autonomous Prefecture, Honghe Hani and Yi Autonomous Prefecture, Ailao Mountain, Wumeng Mountain and Small Liangshan Mountain in northwest Yunnan. They have their own spoken and written lan-

guage and calendar. Fire is the symbol of the Yi's pursuit of light. In Yi areas, the biggest festival is the Torch Festival, always held on the on 24th or 25th of the sixth lunar month. When night falls, people take torches through their fields and villages or sing and dance around huge bonfires.

Yuanmou Earth Forest

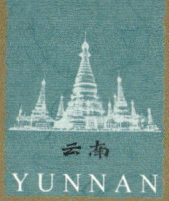

YUNNAN

Luliang Sand Forest

The Yunnan-Burma Road
— "The Last Land Route into China"

If you take a bus in Kunming and travel west via Dali, Baoshan, Luxi and Wanting in Ruili, you will reach the port on the border with Burma. This section is now called National Highway 320; its former incarnation was the Yunnan-Burma Road that was so vital in the Anti-Fascist War in the first half of the 20th century.

In order to connect Yunnan with Burma, in 1924 the provincial authorities started to build the

YUNNAN

Yunnan-Burma Road across western Yunnan. Later, because of the volatility of the political situation, the road edged forward only very slowly. In 1935, the Kunming-Xiaguan section (some 400 km in length) was finally completed. However, after the War of Resistance against Japanese Aggression broke out in 1937, the pace of construction was transformed beyond anyone's imagining.

Since such big commercial ports as Shanghai and Nanjing were facing imminent danger, it became more and more urgent to open a new international transport route to maintain communications with foreign countries. In November 1937 the Chinese Government decided to build a road from Kunming to Wanting in Ruili. As the war was escalating, the project was to be finished in four months. It is not hard to imagine the difficulties — four months to build a road of nearly 550 km through high mountains and lofty ridges of strategic importance and difficult access, plus repairing the already operational 400 km Kunming-Xiaguan section.

From its start in December 1937, more than 200,000 people from a dozen ethnic groups in Yunnan labored on this epic but tragic project. Braving cold winds in high mountains and the high temperatures and miasmas of the low valleys, they used hoes to dig out the mountains, and carried away earth and rock in bamboo baskets, to the light of pine resin torches. The roadworkers' huts

Huitong Bridge on the Yunnan-Burma Highway

stretched for over 500 km along the Xiaguan-Wanting road. According to the then *Yunnan Daily,* between 2,000 and 3,000 workers died on this project.

The Yunnan-Burma Road finally opened to traffic in August 1938; it had taken only nine months for the people of Yunnan to complete this great undertaking. US Ambassador Janson said that the Yunnan-Burma Road was a huge engineering project.... China's completion of this formidable project in such a short period, China's determination, daring and perseverance were really admirable. From a material standpoint the construction of Yunnan-Burma Road had been short of everything: first, it was short of machinery; second, it was purely made by human labor. It all depended on the spirit of fortitude and endurance of people along the road, which far surpassed any nationality in the world....

After the Yunnan-Burma Road opened to traffic, it played a significant role in the Anti-Fascist War, not just for China, but also for the whole of Asia and the Pacific region. It was called "the last land artery into China." Documents show that, between 1938 and 1945, it brought nearly half a million tons of goods and materials into China.

In February 1942, a Chinese expeditionary force of over 100,000 went to Burma along the Yunnan-Burma Road to fight the Japanese fascists. According to a contemporary account, "in the sky there are allied airplanes providing cover; on the ground are vehicle wheels turning and engines roaring. Thousands of vehicles of every kind: tanks, gun carriages, ammunition carriages, infantry transports, ambulances, liaison cars, supply trucks, and British trucks from Burma to help transport soldiers, together forming an enormous steel dragon.... The day the troops set out, people of every ethnic group immediately came out on hearing the news, crowding both sides of the road to give them a send-off. Local headmen placed incense and sacrificial altars according to their local customs... As soon as a truck stopped, people of every ethnic group, men and women, young and old, crowded forward to offer soldiers rice wine and tea.... The road was a sea of people cheering and jumping for joy..."

The Yunnan-Burma Road was the only route out of China at that time. The Japanese flew several hundred aircraft in concentrated bombing raids on the Yunnan-Burma Road where it crossed the Nujiang River at the Huitong Bridge, and the Lancang River at the Gongguo and Changgan bridges. Every time these wood-plank chain bridges sustained bomb damage, they were quickly repaired.

The Flying Tigers and the Hump Route

YUNNAN

Dear Mr. Mayor,

Sixty years ago, the American people, fighting alongside the Chinese people, expelled the enemy from Yunnan. Although victory was achieved, many brave soldiers gave their lives in the fierce struggle. Later, the people of Tengchong built a memorial to commemorate the efforts of the American people at the spot where Chinese officers and men are buried. Today, in this moving commemorative event, people of our two countries are working together to establish the identity of every soldier who died in this struggle, and to rebuild anew the monument that commemorates them.

On behalf of the United States of America, I have the great honor of thanking you for your continuing remembrance of those American soldiers who fell here many years ago.

With my regards and best wishes

Yours, Sincerely
George H. W. Bush

(Note: Translated back from the Chinese translation of the original)

Dressed in special service uniform, "Tiger Cub Joe" a Chinese boy adopted by American forces, in an inspection line-up

- While the Hump Airfield was undergoing rush repairs, the planes were flying "Hump Routes" over perilous terrain under enemy fire.
- The US Air Force "Flying Tigers" inviting a Chinese to try coffee
- Ten airfields in Yunnan were upgraded to allow large planes to land and take off including Kunming, Chenggong, Luliang, Zhanyi, Yangjie, Yunnanyi, and Baoshan.

In September 2004, to commemorate the 19 American soldiers who gave their lives on the western Yunnan front, the people of Tengchong decided to re-erect the memorial to them. When Former US President George Bush, a pilot in World War II, learned about this he asked the writer James Bradley to bring his sincere letter of thanks across the oceans.

Indeed, the 10,000-year-old volcanoes of Tengchong, and the torrential Nujiang and Lancang rivers will never forget the brave war of resistance waged in Yunnan 60 years ago, nor the "Hump Route" opened by American airmen.

In late 1930s, the world Anti-Fascist War was at its height, and the Anti-Japanese War in China was in difficulties.

At that time, retired American General Claire Lee Chennault, who was aviation advisor to the Chinese Government, saw clearly that China, as the major theater of war against Japan, would engage most of the Japanese military, thus helping keep the maximum troop numbers in Europe to fight the Nazis. Since the end of 1930s, General Chennault had been lobbying the White House to offer China air assistance. In 1941, America appropriated 100 fighters from strategic materials meant for Britain, and enrolled several hundred young American volunteers for Kunming.

On December 7, 1941, the Pacific War broke out on all fronts. On December 20, when Japanese bombers came to bomb Kunming again, the fighters of the American Volunteer Group soared into the sky and dealt the Japanese military a devastating blow. The people of Kunming named this outstanding air force the "Flying Tigers," and the

clothes of these aviators were printed with jumping tiger motifs. This was the highest acclaim the Chinese could give a foreign hero.

In July 1942, the Flying Tigers squadron was integrated into the United States Army Air Force's 23rd Fighter Group. In November 1943, a joint squadron of the Chinese and American air forces was established.

In 1942, the Japanese army invaded western Yunnan from Burma and cut off the Yunnan-Burma Road, putting the movement of strategic goods and materials into imminent danger. General Chennault once more put in a request to US President Franklin D. Roosevelt and obtained permission to open an air route from India to China. All Yunnan's ethnic groups were urgently mobilized; huge numbers of people, using the most primitive methods, were poured into the quick expansion of Wujiaba Airport in Kunming and

▶ Japanese fighters of the Fifth Division squadron flew from Myitkyina in Burma targeting Chinese and American "Hump" planes, forcing the "Hump Route" northwards, to the south of the Himalayas. James Dalby, a pilot of the China National Aviation Corporation, began logging the flight status of 62 freight planes of the corporation in 1943. By August 1945, 44 had crashed or gone missing.

▼ Large quantity of materials were transported to Kunming via the "Hump Route," then taken to the front line on trucks, horse-drawn or even man-powered vehicles.

building of a dozen air fields in Chenggong, Yanglin, Luliang, Songming, Yunnanyi and Chuxiong. In May 1942, the same night the Yunnan-Burma Road was cut off by the Japanese army, the famous Hump Route was initiated.

Of all the airlifts in World War II the Hump Route was the most dangerous, the longest in duration and the largest in scale. Starting in India from Dijan airbase in Assam, it flew east over the "Roof of the World" — over the Himalayas, the Gaoligong and the Hengduan mountains, to air fields at Kunming, Yanglin, Luliang and Songming in Yunnan. The route was 550 miles (896 km) long, and about 5,000 m above sea level, the highest elevation being 7,000 m. Performance limitations meant the planes could fly only by a roundabout route that snaked through mountains and valleys. Because of its profile, it was called the Hump Route. The aviators also called it the "Death Route;" due to the atrocious and fickle climate in these areas, planes were always in danger of crashing or colliding, and then there was the Japanese Air Force to beware of....

American post-war statistics show that the US Air Force brought over 800,000 tons of strategic goods into China over "the Hump" within 37 months; the Hump Route claimed 609 US aircraft and 1,500 airmen who died or were posted missing. In this epoch-making airlift, stirring and tragic in equal part, history was created with the blood and the lives of Chinese and American people in the fight for peace.

First Lieutenant Robert H. Mooney

First Lieutenant Robert H. Mooney came to the China battlefield as a volunteer. His group was stationed at the airfield at Yunnanyi, a key town on the Hump Route, charged with defending the airport and escorting transport planes. On December 26, 1942 First Lieutenant Mooney and his fellow airmen took off in their P-40 fighters to engage in-

coming Japanese bombers making a sudden attack on Yunnanyi. The air battle was extremely fierce; fire crimsoned the sky above Yunnanyi airfield and nearby Xiangyun County.

First Lieutenant Mooney shot down an enemy bomber, but another aircraft attacked his P-40 head-on. Mooney went for it fearlessly, and the enemy plane, its left wing damaged, fell and crashed. But Mooney's plane was alight and falling rapidly toward Xiangyun: if it crashed into Xiangyun, it would cause devastation there, as well as affecting Yunnanyi airfield. At the moment of decision Mooney did not bale out; he continued to fly his dying aircraft beyond Xiangyun, not wanting to crash into the center. But by then he was too close to the ground for his parachute to fully open and he was fatally injured when he crash-landed in a field. The people of Xiangyun had witnessed the soul-stirring scene, and all rushed to his rescue. Yunnan's famous Dr Dong Jiyuan used the best drugs and medical skills to save Mooney's life. Sadly, he died from his injuries that same night at Xiangyun.

To commemorate First Lieutenant Mooney, the people of Xiangyun donated money to build a monument in his honor. Each year on the Pure Brightness Festival

◀ First Lieutenant Robert H. Mooney volunteered to fight in China.

▼ 50 years on, Ena I. Davis, Lieutenant Mooney's sister, meeting the old men who had witnessed this history, and their offspring

(April 5), the day that Chinese people commemorate the dead, the people of Xiangyun will recall Mooney in front of this monument before offering sacrifices to their ancestors. In the United States, there is also a monument to First Lieutenant Mooney in North Kansas.

Aircraft 53

On March 11, 1943, the 24-year-old American pilot James R. Fox and Chinese pilots Tan Xuan and Wang Guoliang were flying Transport Aircraft 53 of the China National Aviation Corporation loaded with strategic materials from Wujiaba Airport in Kunming

YUNNAN

to Dijan in India. Aircraft 53 lost connection with ground control when flying over the Gaoligong Mountains in Yunnan. Later another pilot on a mission over Yakou in Pianma among the Gaoligong Mountains, discovered that Aircraft 53 had crashed in a valley. Over the next 50-odd years, China and the United States tried hard to find the wreckage.

On June 3, 1996, a hunter discovered a crashed aircraft at Yakou in Pianma. Finally, a survey of the location and identification of the type and serial number brought the 53-year-long historical mystery of Aircraft 53 to an end. Over the next two years, the Chinese people made superhuman efforts to guard it faithfully; the 24-year-old Qu Tian sacrificed his young life for it, and the dust that once buried James R. Fox covered this young Chinese too.

▌ "Flying Tigers"

On June 10, 1997, the 80-year-old Flying Tigers veteran F. Hanks, after a five-day trek, finally stood, supported by Chinese soldiers and civilians, before the wreckage of Aircraft 53 that his mind had turned to so often over the intervening years. Tears in his eyes, he gave the wing a tender kiss....

The local children made models of Aircraft 53 with azalea leaves growing beside the wreckage. On February 19, 1998, a wooden plaque with models of Aircraft 53 was sent to the San Diego Aerospace Museum in the United States. The museum accepted this precious gift from the east in a solemn ceremony.

On May 27, 1998 the Chinese government moved Aircraft 53 away from its mountain crash site to Pianma Town, some 50 km away. After its 55-year sleep in the mountains, Aircraft 53 was welcomed by the local people in a grand ceremony commemorating both its crew and all those who gave their lives flying the Hump Route.

"Angel of the Hump"

At 5:30 p.m. on March 3, 2004, Dan, a 77-year-old US veteran, knocked at the door of the 92-year-old Huang Huanxiao in Kunming. Once inside, he knelt down on one knee, and addressed her as "Angel of the Hump"....

Huang Huanxiao was the only female nurse in the hospital for the US Air Force Flying Tigers. This was located at Yunnanyi (where the Han Dynasty Emperor Wudi once sent people to find the "rosy clouds appearing in Yunnan." This beautiful and staunch Chinese nurse could not remember how many wounded American military she had tended; what she could remember was "working around the clock," and that "the Flying Tigers were all lovely." When these still immature young fighters, perhaps students, musicians or farmers in civilian life, were brought to the hospital from the front, badly injured or

YUNNAN

Reunion of Huang Huanxiao and pilot Dan of the Flying Tigers

missing an arm or leg, they did not cry or flinch, and bearing the great pain, they would immediately ask, "Can I fly again?" She still remembers that a 21-year-old soldier had his leg amputated, and that as she was giving him an injection, she couldn't help crying. But it was the soldier who comforted her, saying it was all worthwhile since he had shot down three Japanese planes. He also played the violin for this Angel sister... Now, 60 years on, these two old people Huang Huanxiao and Dan, citizens of different nations, cried together, reunited over a vast distance. When bidding farewell, Dan went down on one knee once more...

Time is always the witness and tester of history. Although bloody warfare has been waged in "Shangri-La" — the land of peace and tranquility, Yunnan, this beautiful land of ancient mountains and rivers, homeland of the spirit, remains unchanged across the centuries.

World Exposition

On May 1, 1999, 68 countries took part in the World Horticultural Exposition in Kunming (Expo'99).

The World Horti-Expo Garden runs 2.5 km from east to west, and 1.1 km from north to south, covering an area of 218 ha. Today, the national flags of these 68 countries still flutter at the entrance, the main avenue resplendent with sunshine and flowers, the big flower ship and the towering sign "Blossoming in the New Century," all remain as dazzling as ever.

"Blossoming in the New Century" sculpture

"Man and Nature — Marching into the 21st Century" was the theme of Expo'99, and also a declaration for mankind. Man and nature must live in peace and harmony — losing this balance would be disastrous for both man and Earth. At the entrance of the Man-and-Nature Hall are some words about the earth by Chief Seattle of the Suquamish and other American Indian tribes: "You must remember that it is sacred, you must teach your children that it is sacred.... This we know: the earth does not belong to man; man belongs to the earth. This we all know. All things are connected, like the blood which unites one family. All things are connected."

The World Horti-Expo Garden comprises the China Hall, International Hall, Man-and-Nature Hall, Science and Technology Hall, Grand Greenhouse, Tea Garden, Bonsai Garden, Medicinal Herb Garden, Fruit and Vegetable Garden, Bamboo Garden, Tree Garden, International Exposition Area... The buildings, which reflect the unique styles of each country or province, the rare plants and flowers from all over the world, are all well protected and remain as beautiful as before — perhaps even more vigorous. The garden will take you three days to fully savor.

The World Horticultural Exposition brought forward Kunming's infrastructure building and city development by 10 years. The city also opened four green squares — Jinbi, Wuhuashan, Wuhua and Shengli.

| Flower Avenue

PANORAMIC CHINA

| The International Pavilion

Mystic Land, Diverse Peoples

Nature has no single criterion for life and beauty. In the same Yunnan Province — north, south, east and west, the clouds and rainbows are different; under the same sky — spring, summer, autumn and winter, all have their distinctive features. Wherever in Yunnan you roam, nothing will be bland or dull.

Bamei in Guangnan County
—The "Peach Garden" in a Cave

Bamei village is located less than 40 km from Guangnan County Town.

In order to get to Bamei, you first have to go through a long dark cave on a narrow iron-plated boat. After about an hour, you find yourself in a bright open space: before you, as if by magic, there suddenly appear before your eyes a bridge and a stream, a village and the smoke of cooking fires.

It's like unwittingly stumbling upon a dreamland: an old water mill squeaks with the turning of its wheel; a buffalo boy sits astride an ox; white geese play in the waters of the stream; golden vegetable flowers bloom below the bamboo fences; and the gently rippling Tuoniang River flows beside the village.... Mountains enclose this small world, guarding this sacred place and isolating it from the outside world.

Bamei comes from the Zhuang language, meaning "cave mouth in the forest." The village has 620 or so inhabitants, all of them Zhuang ethnic minority. It was over 300 years ago that they moved here from other parts of China. The senior generation (over sixty-years-old) have hardly ever been out of Bamei.

The people of Bamei lead a self-sufficient life. Neighbors live in harmony; no one picks up and pockets anything lost on the road, and no family needs to bolt their doors at night. Since the people all observe their old ways, no problem involving the police has ever occurred.

This place has its own kind of "civilization" — one of self-sufficiency, peace and serenity.

Source of the Pearl River

The source of south China's Pearl River emerges from a totally unremarkable cave at the foot of Maxiong Mountain in Zhanyi County, Qujing City.

Within the cave, water seeps through cracks in the rocks, flowing out of the cave as the green, clear waters of the Panjiang River. When it flows into Guangxi, its name changes to the Hongshui River, and once in Guangdong Province, it is called the Pearl River.

The discoverer of the source was the famed Ming Dynasty traveler and geographer Xu Xiake, in whom romantic nature and exactitude were combined. He walked to this out-of-

YUNNAN

▲ Source of the Pearl River within the cave
◄ Maxiong Mountain

the-way place and, using his own feet and eyes as his only surveying equipment, came to the conviction that this small stream was the source of the mighty Pearl River. This conclusion is identical with the findings of surveys using modern equipment.

In developing the Pearl River source tourist environment in recent years, the local government and a group of farsighted people have emphasized the importance of cultural development and its irreplaceable role; they set up a "Pearl River Source Memorial Stele" inscribed with lines of glowing literary grace on simple, austere white marble. These, together with poetry in different styles, and brilliant lines by scholars of bygone dynasties, describing the landscape and their feelings, bring a proud quality to the once bleak and desolate Pearl River source.

The Yi Solar Calendar

In remote antiquity, ancestors of the Yi ethnic group living in and around Chuxiong, through observations of the vast, star-crowded skies, of complex and mystical natural phenomena, separated time into seasons that regulated their lives. They divided one year into 10 months according to the solar cycle, which were closely related to farming and animal husbandry. Such was the Yi solar calendar.

As early as the second century BC, Yi people started to settle here and engage in farming. Every year in the sixth and seventh months, heavy rains fell and rivers in mountain valleys breached their banks; in the ninth and tenth months when the floods retreated, the Yi ancestors would plant crops on the riverbanks, which they would harvest in the third and fourth months of the next year. In order to farm in the right season, they gradually came to understand they had to know the rainy season and the dry seasons, the time for sowing and the time harvesting. They also found that these were closely linked to the "walking" of the sun. They carved on wooden stakes or walls the time when things flowered and when they died, when tides peaked and when they were at their lowest, establishing that there were about 365 days between these two natural phenomena. There is less than six hours difference between this and the time it takes for the earth to orbit the sun, as measured by modern science — 365 days 5 hours 48 minutes and 46 seconds, to be precise.

YUNNAN

According to the Yi solar calendar, every month was divided into 36 days. After the 10 months, the remaining five or six days were defined as "New Year Days." The "New Year Days" would usually be five days, and six every fourth year.

Although the Yi 10-month solar calendar did not spread very far afield, the ancient wisdom, civilization and creativity it embodies will shine forever.

The majestic 10-month Solar Calendar Plaza in Chuxiong, the capital of Yi Autonomous Prefecture, covers an area of 5,220.4 sq m. It is a monument to the ancient pioneering work of the Yi people.

The plaza is round, designed to reflect the ancient Yi sacrificial altar of Heaven (an observatory where the Yi ancestors determined the four seasons according to the sun's rotation and the constellations). It is divided into three tiered terraces, 18.3 m high in total, with 40 carved reliefs relating three beautiful Yi folktales.

Majestic Pass on the Wumeng Mountains

Walking into the towering Wumeng Mountains in Shaotong, you see meandering, lofty, and sheer mountain ranges stretching hundreds of kilometers long, fantastic peaks and steep cliffs, chain after chain of them. As described in the poem of Chairman Mao Zedong, "The majestic Wumeng roll by, globules of clay." Such boldness of vision and heart!

It was in this "awesome" land that, one step at a time, its ancient people first walked the Wuchi or Five-Foot Road.

The Five-Foot Road, built during the Warring States Period (475 BC-221 BC), Qin (221 BC-206 BC) and Han (206 BC-220 AD) dynasties, starts at Chengdu in Sichuan Province, goes through Yibin in southern Sichuan, before entering Yunnan via the meandering and boundless Wumeng Mountains in Zhaotong. It was a vital route from Yunnan into Sichuan and the Central Plains.

There is one Place on the Five-Foot Road that people must go through—the Dousha Pass. For thousands of years, down the generations, caravans have come and gone by day and by night. During the Tang Dynasty it was known as Shimen Pass, the river below was called Guanhe. Because of the terrain, the gateway at Dousha Pass is not a big one and the gray flagstone road has

◄ Wumeng Mountains
► Horse tracks on the Five-Foot Road

to thread through the gateway perched on the edge of the cliff. Look down from the pass gateway, and you will see trains and buses coming and going on the banks of today's Guan River. The Neijiang-Kunming Railway goes right into the depths of these misty, vast mountains, leaving the majestic wind- and rain-weathered Dousha Pass to safeguard its ages old history.

It is the horse footprints on the steep flagstone path that have been taken by numerous cameras and videos. How many caravans it must have taken to leave such deep prints on this winding stone-path over thousands of years.

Below the Dousha Pass is Dousha Town, replete with the atmosphere of those days. There are old streets, shabby houses with green-gray rooftiles and wooden shopfronts. Men in white caps, with long-stemmed Chinese pipes dangling from their lips, sit leisurely and carefree at the teahouses' highly polished "Eight Immortals" tables When business is slack, the proprietress of the cold spicy noodle shop next door, will painstakingly sew the soles of old-fashioned cloth shoes, stitch by stitch. Roadside stalls put out block-printed *24 Examples of Filial Piety, Commandments for Women, Lu Ban's Manual of Carpentry and Exhortations to People*.... The people here believe in traditional Chinese morality.

People carrying goods on their back in horn-shaped baskets to rural markets pass through the Dousha Pass on their way to the town. They don't have time even to look at those deep horse footprints and inscriptions on the cliffs. The questions of who wrote those cliff-face words and how many soldiers guarded the Dousha Pass are irrelevant to their lives: today they will sell piglets and sweet potatoes, and buy salt and tobacco. Life is like the river below the mountain, carrying on making the same sounds, doing the same thing.

It is this "carefreeness" that makes the lifestyle and history of this locality emerge in such a natural way.

Ethnic Minorities Found Only in Yunnan

Achang

Jino

Blang

De'ang

YUNNAN

Lahu

Va

Nu

Pumi

Lisu

Jingpo

Dai

Derung

YUNNAN

Naxi

Bai

Hani

Appendixes

Appendix I: Ethnic Minority Festivals in Yunnan

Ethnic Group	Festival	Lunar Calendar	Place(s)	Activities
Yi	Tiger Festival	The 8th to 15th of the 1st month	Xiaomaidichong Village in Shuangbai County	Dancing
	Flower-Arranging Festival/Dage (Song & Dance) Festival	The 8th of the 2nd month	Dayao, and Shuangjiang	Picking and arranging azaleas
	Mizhi Festival	The 8th of the 2nd month	Stone Forest	Offering sacrifices to the Dragon Tree, picnics
	Dragon Festival	The 8th of the 2nd month	Jinggu	Lusheng Dance
	March Market	The 28th of the 3rd month	Mouding	Country fair, dancing
	Clothing Festival	The 28th of the 3rd month	Dayao	Dress competition
	Torchlight Festival	The 24th to 25th of the 6th month	Stone Forest, Chuxiong, and Dali	Torchlight, bullfighting, wrestling, singing and dancing
Bai	March Fair	The 14th to 16th of the 3rd month	Dali	Trading, horse racing, dragon-boat race, singing and dancing
	Raosanling	The 23rd to 25th of the 4th month	Dali	Mountain circumambulation, offering sacrifices to ancestors, dancing
	Torchlight Festival	The 25th of the 6th month	Dali	Praying for good fortune and bumper harvests
	Shibao Mountain Song Festival	3 days between the end of the 7th month and the start of the 8th month	Jianchuan	Playing and singing Bai love songs
	Benzhu (Patron God) Festival	No fixed date	Dali	Worshipping Patron God, chanting scriptures
Naxi	Sanduo Festival	The 8th of the 2nd month	Lijiang	Horse racing, dancing, picnic
	Mule and Horse Fair	One week, from the 7th of the 7th month	At the foot of the Lion Mountain in Lijiang	Livestock fair
	Mila/Bangbang Fair	The 15th of the fifth month	Lijiang	Farming fair, horse racing
	July Fair	The middle 10 days of the 7th month	Lijiang	Big livestock fair, antiphonal singing
	Heaven-Worshiping	No fixed date	Lijiang	Praying for good fortune and a bumper harvest
Miao	Flower Mountain Festival	The 3rd of the 1st month	Pingbian, and Yongshan	Climbing the flower pole, singing and dancing
Mosuo	Mountain Worshiping Festival	The 25th of the 7th month	Lugu Lake	Offering sacrifices to the Goddess, singing and dancing, archery, searching for lovers
Jingpo	Munao Zongge (Song & Dance) Festival	The 15th of the 1st month	Luxi, and Longchuan	Dancing

Tibetan	Buddhahood Attaining Day	The 1st to 4th of the 4th month	Dechen, and Zhongdian	Offering sacrifices
	Horse-Race Festival	The 5th of the 5th month	Zhongdian Pastureland	Horse racing, banquet, picnic
	Duanyang Festival	The 5th of the 5th month	Dechen	Horse racing, singing and dancing, banquet
	Buddha's Enlightenment Day	The 25th of the 10th month	Dechen, and Zhongdian	Offering sacrifices
	Evil-Exorcising Dance Ceremony	New Year's Eve in Tibetan Calendar	Dechen	Dancing to exorcise evil spirits
Bouyei	Ox King Festival	The 8th of the 4th month	Luoping, and Fuyuan	Feeding food to oxen, eating Ox King Cake, singing and dancing
Dai	Dragon-Worshipping Festival	January in Solar Calendar	Xishuangbanna	Offering sacrifices to the Dragon God
	Picking Flowers Day	April in Solar Calendar	Jinggu	Picking flowers for Buddha
	Water-Splashing Festival	The mid 4th month of Solar Calendar	Xishuangbanna, and Dehong	Water-splashing, lighting *Gaosheng* rockets, dragon-boat race, singing and dancing
Hani	Zhalizuo Festival	The 1st of the 1st month	Mojiang	Offering sacrifices to ancestors, antiphonal singing, banquet
	Girls' Festival	The 2nd of the 2nd month	Honghe	Picnic, singing and dancing
	Amatu Festival	The dragon day of the 2nd month	Jinping	Offering sacrifices to mountains and ancestors, etc.
	Mothers Festival	The 1st ox day of the 3rd month	Simao	Offering sacrifices to mothers, singing in memory of mothers
	Kuzhazha Festival	The 6th month	Honghe	Offering sacrifices to gods, singing and dancing
	New Rice Festival	The 1st and 2nd dragon days of the 8th month	Honghe	Tasting new rice, offering sacrifices to Heaven, ancestors and the dead
	Zhalete Festival	Within the middle 10 days of the 10th month	Simao, and Honghe	Offering sacrifices to ancestors, long-street banquet
Zhuang	Longduan Festival	The 3rd month	Funing	Trade fair, young people's social gathering, antiphonal singing
Lisu	Bathing Festival	Spring Festival	Dechen	Bathing, making friends
	Sword Pole Festival	The 8th of the 2nd month	Nujiang, and Baoshan	Climbing the blade mountain
	Singing Festival	The 12th month or the first 10 days of the 1st month	Nujiang	Singing contest, bathing
Hui	Lesser Bairam	The 1st of the 10th month in Moslem Calendar	Kunming and other places	Religious services, etc.
	Corban Festival	The 12th month in Moslem Calendar	Kunming and other places	Mass worship, killing ox or sheep, etc.
Lahu	Kuoshi Festival	The 1st of the 1st month	Lancang, and Menglian	Receiving new water, Lusheng Dance, hunting
	Worshiping the Sun God	The Beginning of Summer	Lancang County	Worshiping gods, praying for a bumper harvest
	Calabash Festival	The 10th month	Lancang	Trade fair, Lusheng Dance
Va	Festival of Pulling the Wooden Drum	The 12th month	Ximeng, and Cangyuan	Pulling the wooden drum, dancing, bull piercing
Nu	Flower Festival	The 15th of the 3rd month	Nujiang River valley	Picking fresh flowers, offering sacrifices to fairies
	Nu New Year	The 29th of the 12th month	Nujiang River valley	Archery, dancing

Appendix II: Major Hotels in Yunnan

Kunming

Name	Grade	Address	Telephone Number
Kai Wah Plaza International Hotel	Five-star	157 Beijing Lu, Kunming	0871-3562828
Kunming Bank Hotel	Five-star	399 Qingnian Lu, Kunming	0871-3158888
Kunming Harbor Plaza Hotel	Five-star	20 Honghua Qiao, Kunming	0871-5386688
Horizon Hotel	Five-star	432 Qingnian Lu, Kunming	0871-3186666
Kunming Hotel	Four-star	52 Dongfeng Donglu, Kunming	0871-3162063
King World Hotel	Four-star	98 Beijing Lu, Kunming	0871-3138888
Golden Dragon Hotel	Four-star	575 Beijing Lu, Kunming	0871-3133015
Holiday Inn Kunming	Four-star	25 Dongfeng Donglu, Kunming	0871-3165888
Courtyard by Marriott Kunming	Four-star	300 Huancheng Xilu, Kunming	0871-4158888
Green Lake Hotel	Four-star	6 Cuihu Nanlu, Kunming	0871-5158888
Green Land Hotel	Four-star	80 Tuodong Lu, Kunming	0871-3189999
New Era Hotel	Four-star	99 Dongfeng Xilu, Kunming	0871-3625999

Xishuangbanna

Name	Grade	Address	Telephone Number
Dai Garden Hotel	Four-star	8 Nonglin Nanlu, Jinghong, Xishuangbanna	0691-2130558
Crown Hotel	Three-star	Tourism & Holiday District, Jinghong, Xishuangbanna	0691-2128888
New International Hotel	Three-star	2 Jingde Donglu, Jinghong, Xishuangbanna	0691-2126888
Chai Xin Hotel	Three-star	Tourism & Holiday District, Jinghong, Xishuangbanna	0691-2139888
Dalian Hotel Xishuangbanna	Three-star	3rd Lu, Tourism & Holiday District, Jinghong, Xishuangbanna	0691-2130999
Golden Phoenix Hotel	Three-star	Tourism & Holiday District, Jinghong, Xishuangbanna	0691-2129888
Yintong Mansion	Three-star	1st Lu, Tourism & Holiday District, Jinghong, Xishuangbanna	0691-2149888

Dali

Name	Grade	Address	Telephone Number
Dali Asia Star Hotel	Four-star	Tourism & Holiday District, South of Old Town, Dali	0872-2670009
Manwan Hotel	Four-star	Canglang Lu, Dali	0872-2181739
Dali Cangshan Hotel	Three-star	118 Cangshan Lu, Dali	0872-2171666
Xiaguan Hotel	Three-star	1 Renmin Beilu, Dali	0872-2125579

Lijiang

Name	Grade	Address	Telephone Number
Lijiang Guanfang Hotel	Four-star	Shangri-la Dadao, Lijiang	0888-518888
Black and White River Hotel	Three-star	Huancheng Nanlu, Dayan Town, Lijiang County	0888-5126688
Lijiang Grand Hotel	Three-star	Xinyi Jie, Dayan Town, Lijiang County	0888-5128888
Lijiang Senlong Hotel	Three-star	Minsheng Lu, Lijiang County	0888-5120666

Appendix III: World Cultural and Natural Heritage Sites in Yunnan

Name	Approved Date	Category
The Old Town of Lijiang	December 1997	Cultural
Three Parallel Rivers of Yunnan Protected Areas	July 2003	Natural

Appendix IV: State-Level Scenic Spots in Yunnan

Stone Forest in Lunan; Dali; Xishuangbanna; Three Parallel Rivers of Yunnan Protected Areas; Dianchi Lake in Kunming; the Yulong (Jade Dragon) Snow Mountain in Lijiang; volcanoes and hot springs in Tengchong; Ruili River—Daying River; Jiuxiang Karst Caves in Yiliang; and Jianshui

Appendix V: Famous State-Level Historical and Cultural Cities/Towns in Yunnan

Kunming, Dali, Weishan, Lijiang, Jianshui

Appendix VI: Related Websites

Yunnan Provincial Tourism Administration: www.tourinfo.com.cn
Yunnan Tourism Information Center: www.traveloyunnan.com.cn
Yunnan Tourism Website: www.yunnanhotels.com/yunnantravel/index.html
Information Office of Yunnan Provincial People's Government: www.yunnan.cn

▲ At the Lancang River

◀ Yi folksong and folkdance

▲ Dongba totem pictures
◀ The Dai people follow Hinayana Buddhism.
◀ Clouds over Lugu Lake

图书在版编目（CIP）数据

云南：云天之外的香格里拉 / 云南省人民政府新闻办公室主编.
北京：外文出版社, 2005 (全景中国)
ISBN 7-119-04077-4
I. 云... II. 云... III. 民族文化 - 简介 - 云南省 - 英文 IV.K280.74
中国版本图书馆 CIP 数据核字（2005）第 054976 号

全景中国— 云南：云天之外的香格里拉

主　　编：云南省人民政府新闻办公室
撰　　稿：欧之德
图片提供：刘建明　邢　毅　倪　永　张少明　刘建华　曾宪华　赵　汀　杨骏彪
　　　　　杨惠滇　夏碧辉　肖依群　云南省人民政府新闻办公室

英文翻译：张韶宁　李　洋　王　琴　欧阳伟萍　冯　鑫
英文审定：唐　素　郁　苓

中文审定：过桔新
责任编辑：杨春燕
装帧设计：蔡　荣
内文设计：奇文云海
印刷监制：韩少乙

© 2006 外文出版社
出版发行：
外文出版社（中国北京百万庄大街 24 号）
邮政编码 100037　http://www.flp.com.cn
制　　版：
外文出版社照排中心
印　　制：
北京京都六环印刷厂
开本：980mm × 710mm 1/16（平装） 印张：19
2006 年第 1 版第 1 次印刷
（英）
ISBN 7-119-04077-4
09800
85-E-579P

版权所有　侵权必究